Hands-On Machine Learning with ML.NET

Getting started with Microsoft ML.NET to implement popular machine learning algorithms in C#

Jarred Capellman

BIRMINGHAM - MUMBAI

Hands-On Machine Learning with ML.NET

Commissioning Editor: Pravin Dhandre
Acquisition Editor: Devika Battike
Content Development Editor: Joseph Sunil
Senior Editor: David Sugarman
Technical Editor: Utkarsha Kadam
Copy Editor: Safis Editing
Project Coordinator: Aishwarya Mohan
Proofreader: Safis Editing
Indexer: Manju Arasan
Production Designer: Aparna Bhagat

First published: March 2020

Production reference: 2280820

Published by Packt Publishing Ltd.
Livery Place
35 Livery Street
Birmingham
B3 2PB, UK.

ISBN 978-1-78980-178-1

www.packt.com

To my amazing wife, Amy, for completing me.

– Jarred Capellman

Why subscribe?

- Spend less time learning and more time coding with practical eBooks and Videos from over 4,000 industry professionals

- Improve your learning with Skill Plans built especially for you

- Get a free eBook or video every month

- Fully searchable for easy access to vital information

- Copy and paste, print, and bookmark content

Contributors

About the author

Jarred Capellman is a Director of Engineering at SparkCognition, a cutting-edge artificial intelligence company located in Austin, Texas. At SparkCognition, he leads the engineering and data science team on the industry-leading machine learning endpoint protection product, DeepArmor, combining his passion for software engineering, cybersecurity, and data science. In his free time, he enjoys contributing to GitHub daily on his various projects and is working on his DSc in cybersecurity, focusing on applying machine learning to solving network threats. He currently lives just outside of Austin, Texas, with his wife, Amy.

To my wife, Amy, who supported me through the nights and weekends – I devote this book to her.

About the reviewer

Andrew Greenwald holds an MSc in computer science from Drexel University and a BSc in electrical engineering with a minor in mathematics from Villanova University. He started his career designing solid-state circuits to test electronic components. For the past 25 years, he has been developing software for IT infrastructure, financial markets, and defense applications. He is currently applying machine learning to cybersecurity, developing models to detect zero-day malware. Andrew lives in Austin, Texas, with his wife and three sons.

Packt is searching for authors like you

If you're interested in becoming an author for Packt, please visit `authors.packtpub.com` and apply today. We have worked with thousands of developers and tech professionals, just like you, to help them share their insight with the global tech community. You can make a general application, apply for a specific hot topic that we are recruiting an author for, or submit your own idea.

Table of Contents

Section 2: ML.NET Models

Preface

Machine learning (ML) is widely used in many industries, such as science, healthcare, and research and its popularity is only growing. In March 2018, Microsoft introduced ML.NET to help .NET enthusiasts to work with ML. With this book, you'll explore how to build ML.NET applications with the various ML models available using C# code.

The book starts by giving you an overview of ML and the types of ML algorithms used, along with covering what ML.NET is and why you need it to build ML apps. You'll then explore the ML.NET framework, its components, and APIs. The book will serve as a practical guide to helping you build smart apps using the ML.NET library. You'll gradually become well-versed in how to implement ML algorithms such as regression, classification, and clustering with real-world examples and datasets. Each chapter will cover the practical implementation, showing you how to implement ML within .NET applications. You'll also learn how to integrate TensorFlow into ML.NET applications. Later, you'll discover how to store the regression model housing price prediction results in the database and display the real-time predicted results from the database on your web application using ASP.NET Core Blazor and SignalR.

By the end of this book, you'll have learned how to confidently perform basic to advanced-level machine learning tasks in ML.NET.

Who this book is for

If you are a .NET developer who wants to implement machine learning models using ML.NET, then this book is for you. This book will also be beneficial to data scientists and machine learning developers who are looking for effective tools to implement various machine learning algorithms. A basic understanding of C# and .NET is mandatory to grasp the concepts covered in this book effectively.

What this book covers

Chapter 1, *Getting Started with Machine Learning and ML.NET*, talks about what machine learning is and how important machine learning is in our society today. It also introduces ML.NET and talks in more detail about getting started with it after learning about the concepts of machine learning and how they relate.

Chapter 2, *Setting Up the ML.NET Environment*, talks in more detail about getting started with ML.NET, continuing the overview of machine learning and how ML.NET can assist in both developing and running models in both new and existing applications. You will ensure your development environment is set up and the chapter ends with a simple pre-trained model in a console application to demonstrate that you are ready to proceed with the training.

Chapter 3, *Regression Model*, talks about using a regression and logistic regression model in ML.NET in addition to the math and what problems these models can help to solve. In addition, the chapter provides a step-by-step explanation of how to create and work with both a regression model and a logistic regression model in ML.NET. The end of the chapter details a quick console application using the dataset and both the models in ML.NET.

Chapter 4, *Classification Model*, talks about using the classifications trainer models in ML.NET and what problems a classification model can help to solve. For this chapter, we will create two applications to demonstrate the classification trainer support in ML.NET. The first predicts whether a car is of good value based on the several attributes and comparative prices using the FastTree trainer that ML.NET provides. The second application takes email data (Subject, Body, Sender) with the SDCA trainer in ML.NET to classify the email as an Order, Spam or Friend. Through these applications, you will also learn how to evaluate classification models.

Chapter 5, *Clustering Model*, talks about using the k-means clustering trainer in ML.NET in addition to what problems a clustering model can help to solve. In this chapter, we will use the k-means cluster trainer that ML.NET provides in order to create an example application that will classify files as either executables, documents, or scripts. In addition, you will learn how to evaluate clustering models in ML.NET.

Chapter 6, *Anomaly Detection Model*, talks about using an anomaly detection model in ML.NET in addition to what problems an anomaly detection model can help to solve. For this chapter, we will create two example applications. The first uses ML.NET with SSA to detect Network Traffic anomalies, while the second example uses ML.NET with PCA to detect anomalies in a series of user logins. With these applications, we will also look at how you can evaluate your anomaly detection model once trained.

Chapter 7, *Matrix Factorization Model*, talks about using a matrix factorization model in ML.NET in addition to the math and what problems a matrix factorization model can help to solve. In this chapter, we will create a music recommendation application using the matrix factorization trainer that ML.NET provides. Using several data points this recommendation engine will recommend music based on the training data provided to the model. In addition, after creating this application we will learn how to evaluate a matrix factorization model in ML.NET.

Chapter 8, *Using ML.NET with .NET Core and Forecasting*, covers a real-world application utilizing .NET Core and utilizes both a regression and time series model to demonstrate forecasting on stock shares.

Chapter 9, *Using ML.NET with ASP.NET Core*, covers a real-world application utilizing ASP.NET with a frontend to upload a file to determine whether it is malicious or not. This chapter focuses on using a binary classifier and how to integrate it into an ASP.NET application.

Chapter 10, *Using ML.NET with UWP*, covers a real-world application utilizing UWP and ML.NET. The application will utilize ML.NET to classify whether the web page content is malicious. The chapter will also cover UWP application design and MVVM briefly to give a true production-ready sample app to build on or adapt to other applications for using UWP with ML.NET.

Chapter 11, *Training and Building Production Models*, covers training a model at scale with all of the considerations, along with the proper training of a production model using the DMTP project. The lessons learned include obtaining proper training sets (diversity being key), proper features, and the true evaluation of your model. The focus of this chapter is on tips, tricks, and best practices for training production-ready models.

Chapter 12, *Using TensorFlow with ML.NET*, talks about using a pre-trained TensorFlow model with ML.NET to determine whether a car is in a picture or not with a UWP application.

Chapter 13, *Using ONNX with ML.NET*, talks about using a pre-trained ONNX model with ML.NET in addition to the value added by taking a pre-existing ONNX format model into ML.NET directly.

To get the most out of this book

You will need a version of Angular installed on your computer—the latest version, if possible. All code examples have been tested using Angular 9 on Windows OS. However, they should work with future version releases too.

Software/Hardware covered in the book	OS Requirements
Microsoft Visual Studio 2019	A common Windows 10 development environment with 20-50 GB of free space (a quad core processor and 8 GB of RAM is highly recommended)

If you are using the digital version of this book, we advise you to type the code yourself or access the code via the GitHub repository (link available in the next section). Doing so will help you avoid any potential errors related to the copy/pasting of code.

Download the example code files

You can download the example code files for this book from your account at www.packt.com. If you purchased this book elsewhere, you can visit www.packtpub.com/support and register to have the files emailed directly to you.

You can download the code files by following these steps:

1. Log in or register at www.packt.com.
2. Select the **Support** tab.
3. Click on **Code Downloads**.
4. Enter the name of the book in the **Search** box and follow the onscreen instructions.

Once the file is downloaded, please make sure that you unzip or extract the folder using the latest version of:

- WinRAR/7-Zip for Windows
- Zipeg/iZip/UnRarX for Mac
- 7-Zip/PeaZip for Linux

The code bundle for the book is also hosted on GitHub
at https://github.com/PacktPublishing/Hands-On-Machine-Learning-with-ML.NET. In
case there's an update to the code, it will be updated on the existing GitHub repository.

We also have other code bundles from our rich catalog of books and videos available
at https://github.com/PacktPublishing/. Check them out!

Download the color images

We also provide a PDF file that has color images of the screenshots/diagrams used in this
book. You can download it
here: http://www.packtpub.com/sites/default/files/downloads/9781789801781_ColorI
mages.pdf.

Conventions used

There are a number of text conventions used throughout this book.

CodeInText: Indicates code words in text, database table names, folder names, filenames,
file extensions, pathnames, dummy URLs, user input, and Twitter handles. Here is an
example: "The first time the application is run, the ML.NET version of the model is trained
with the images and tags.tsv file (to be reviewed in the next section)."

A block of code is set as follows:

```
public void Classify(string imagePath)
{
    var result = _prediction.Predict(imagePath);

    ImageClassification = $"Image ({imagePath}) is a picture of
{result.PredictedLabelValue} with a confidence of
{result.Score.Max().ToString("P2")}";
}
```

When we wish to draw your attention to a particular part of a code block, the relevant lines
or items are set in bold:

```
dotnet --version
3.0.100
```

Bold: Indicates a new term, an important word, or words that you see onscreen. For
example, words in menus or dialog boxes appear in the text like this. Here is an example:
"Firstly, ensure that **.NET desktop development**, **Universal Windows Platform
Development**, and **ASP.NET and web development** are checked."

Warnings or important notes appear like this.

 Tips and tricks appear like this.

Get in touch

Feedback from our readers is always welcome.

General feedback: If you have questions about any aspect of this book, mention the book title in the subject of your message and email us at customercare@packtpub.com.

Errata: Although we have taken every care to ensure the accuracy of our content, mistakes do happen. If you have found a mistake in this book, we would be grateful if you would report this to us. Please visit www.packtpub.com/support/errata, selecting your book, clicking on the Errata Submission Form link, and entering the details.

Piracy: If you come across any illegal copies of our works in any form on the Internet, we would be grateful if you would provide us with the location address or website name. Please contact us at copyright@packt.com with a link to the material.

If you are interested in becoming an author: If there is a topic that you have expertise in and you are interested in either writing or contributing to a book, please visit authors.packtpub.com.

Reviews

Please leave a review. Once you have read and used this book, why not leave a review on the site that you purchased it from? Potential readers can then see and use your unbiased opinion to make purchase decisions, we at Packt can understand what you think about our products, and our authors can see your feedback on their book. Thank you!

For more information about Packt, please visit packt.com.

Section 1: Fundamentals of Machine Learning and ML.NET

This section gives an overview of this book's audience and a short introduction to machine learning and the importance of learning how to utilize machine learning. In addition, this section introduces the reader to ML.NET. It also talks about the tools and framework needed to build the applications and gives a step-by-step explanation of how to work with ML.NET.

This section comprises the following chapters:

- Chapter 1, *Getting Started with Machine Learning and ML.NET*
- Chapter 2, *Setting Up the ML.NET Environment*

1
Getting Started with Machine Learning and ML.NET

By opening this book, you are taking the first step in disrupting your own knowledge by approaching solutions to complex problems with machine learning. You will be achieving this with the use of Microsoft's ML.NET framework. Having spent several years applying machine learning to cybersecurity, I'm confident that the knowledge you garner from this book will not only open career opportunities to you but also open up your thought processes and change the way you approach problems. No longer will you even approach a complex problem without thinking about how machine learning could possibly solve it.

Over the course of this book, you will learn about the following:

- How and when to use five different algorithms that ML.NET provides
- Real-world end-to-end examples demonstrating ML.NET algorithms
- Best practices when training your models, building your training sets, and feature engineering
- Using pre-trained models in both TensorFlow and ONNX formats

This book does assume that you have a reasonably solid understanding of C#. If you have other experience with a strongly typed object-oriented programming language such as C++ or Java, the syntax and design patterns are similar enough to not hinder your ability to follow the book. However, if this is your first deep dive into a strongly typed language such as C#, I strongly suggest picking up *Learn C# in 7 Days*, by Gaurav Aroraa, published by Packt Publishing, to get a quick foundation. In addition, no prior machine learning experience is required or expected, although a cursory understanding will accelerate your learning.

In this chapter, we will cover the following:

- The importance of learning about machine learning today
- The model-building process
- Exploring types of learning
- Exploring various machine learning algorithms
- Introduction to ML.NET

By the end of the chapter, you should have a fundamental understanding of what it takes to build a model from start to finish, providing the basis for the remainder of the book.

The importance of learning about machine learning today

In recent years, machine learning and artificial intelligence have become an integral part of many of our lives in use cases as diverse as finding cancer cells in an MRI and facial and object recognition during a professional basketball game. Over the course of just the four years between 2013 and 2017, machine learning patents alone grew 34%, while spending is estimated to grow to $57.6B by 2021 (`https://www.forbes.com/sites/louiscolumbus/ 2018/02/18/roundup-of-machine-learning-forecasts-and-market-estimates-2018/ #794d6f6c2225`).

Despite its status as a growing technology, the term machine learning was coined back in 1959 by Arthur Samuel—so what caused the 60-year gap before its adoption? Perhaps the two most significant factors were the availability of technology able to process model predictions fast enough, and the amount of data being captured every minute digitally. According to DOMO Inc, a study in 2017 concluded that 2.5 quintillion bytes were generated daily and that at that time, 90% of the world's data was created between 2015 and 2017 (`https://www.domo.com/learn/data-never-sleeps-5?aid=ogsm072517_1 sf100871281=1`). By 2025, it is estimated that 463 exabytes of data are going to be created daily (`https://www.visualcapitalist.com/how-much-data-is-generated-each-day/`), much of which will come from cars, videos, pictures, IoT devices, emails, and even devices that have not made the transition to the smart movement yet.

The amount that data has grown in the last decade has led to questions about how a business or corporation can use such data for better sales forecasting, anticipating a customer's needs, or detecting malicious bytes in a file. Traditional statistical approaches could potentially require exponentially more staff to keep up with current demands, let alone scale with the data captured. Take, for instance, Google Maps. With Google's acquisition of Waze in 2013, users of Google Maps have been provided with extremely accurate routing suggestions based on the anonymized GPS data of its users. With this model, the more data points (in this case GPS data from smartphones), the better predictions Google can make for your travel. As we will discuss later in this chapter, quality datasets are a critical component of machine learning, especially in the case of Google Maps, where, without a proper dataset, the user experience would be subpar.

In addition, the speed of computer hardware, specifically specialized hardware tailored for machine learning, has also played a role. The use of **Application-Specific Integrated Circuits (ASICs)** has grown exponentially. One of the most popular ASICs on the market is the Google **Tensor Processing Unit (TPU)**. Originally released in 2016, it has since gone through two iterations and provides cloud-based acceleration for machine learning tasks on Google Cloud Platform. Other cloud platforms, such as Amazon's AWS and Microsoft's Azure, also provide FPGAs.

Additionally, **Graphics Processing Units (GPUs)** from both AMD and NVIDIA are accelerating both cloud-based and local workloads, with ROCm Platform and CUDA-accelerated libraries respectively. In addition to accelerated workloads, typical professional GPUs offered by AMD and NVIDIA provide a much higher density of processors than the traditional CPU-only approach. For instance, the AMD Radeon Instinct MI60 provides 4,096 stream processors. While not a full-fledged x86 core, it is not a one-to-one comparison, and the peak performance of double-precision floating-point tasks is rated at 7.373 TFLOPs compared to the 2.3 TFLOPs in AMD's extremely powerful EPYC 7742 server CPU. From a cost and scalability perspective, utilizing GPUs in even a workstation configuration would provide an exponential reduction in training time if the algorithms were accelerated to take advantage of the more specialized cores offered by AMD and NVIDIA. Fortunately, ML.NET provides GPU acceleration with little additional effort.

From a software engineering career perspective, with this growth and demand far outpacing the supply, there has never been a better time to develop machine learning skills as a software engineer. Furthermore, software engineers also possess skills that traditional data scientists do not have – for instance, being able to automate tasks such as the model building process rather than relying on manual scripts. Another example of where a software engineer can provide more value is by adding both unit tests and efficacy tests as part of the full pipeline when training a model. In a large production application, having these automated tests is critical to avoid production issues.

Finally, in 2018, for the first time ever, data was considered more valuable than oil. As industries continue to adopt the use of data gathering and existing industries take advantage of the data they have, machine learning will be intertwined with the data. Machine learning to data is what refining plants are to oil.

The model building process

Before diving into ML.NET, an understanding of core machine learning concepts is required. These concepts will help create a foundation for you to build on as we start building models and learning the various algorithms ML.NET provides over the course of this book. At a high level, producing a model is a complex process; however, it can be broken down into six main steps:

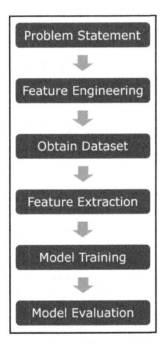

Over the next few sections, we will go through each of these steps in detail to provide you with a clear understanding of how to perform each step and how each step relates to the overall machine learning process as a whole.

Defining your problem statement

Effectively, what problem are you attempting to solve? Being specific at this point is crucial as a less concise problem can lead to considerable re-work. For example, take the following problem statement: *Predicting the outcome of an election*. My first question upon hearing that problem statement would be, at what level? County, state, or national? Each level more than likely requires considerably more features and data to properly predict than the last. A better problem statement, especially early on in your machine learning journey, would be for a specific position at a county level, such as *Predicting the 2020 John Doe County Mayor*. With this more direct problem statement, your features and dataset are much more focused and more than likely attainable. Even with more experience in machine learning, proper scoping of your problem statement is critical. The five Ws of Who, What, When, Where, and Why should be followed to keep your statement concise.

Defining your features

The second step in machine learning is defining your features. Think of features as components or attributes of the problem you wish to solve. In machine learning – specifically, when creating a new model – features are one of the biggest impacts on your model's performance. Properly thinking through your problem statement will promote an initial set of features that will drive differentiation between your dataset and model results. Going back to the Mayor example in the preceding section, what features would you consider data points for the citizen? Perhaps start by looking at the Mayor's competition and where he/she sits on issues in ways that differ from other candidates. These values could be turned into features and then made into a poll for citizens of John Doe County to answer. Using these data points would create a solid first pass at features. One aspect here that is also found in model building is running several iterations of feature engineering and model training, especially as your dataset grows. After model evaluation, *feature importance* is used to determine what features are actually driving your predictions. Occasionally, you will find that gut-instinct features can actually be inconsequential after a few iterations of model training and feature engineering.

In Chapter 11, *Training and Building Production Models*, we will deep dive into best practices when defining features and common approaches to complex problems to obtain a solid first pass at feature engineering.

Obtaining a dataset

As you can imagine, one of the most important aspects of the model building process is obtaining a high-quality dataset. A dataset is used to train the model on what the output should be in the case of the aforementioned case of supervised learning. In the case of unsupervised learning, labeling is required for the dataset. A common misconception when creating a dataset is that bigger is better. This is far from the truth in a lot of cases. Continuing the preceding example, what if all of the poll results answered the same way for every single question? At that point, your dataset is composed of all the same data points and your model will not be able to properly predict any of the other candidates. This outcome is called *overfitting*. A diverse but representative dataset is required for machine learning algorithms to properly build a production-ready model.

In Chapter 11, *Training and Building Production Models*, we will deep dive into the methodology of obtaining quality datasets, looking at helpful resources, ways to manage your datasets, and transforming data, commonly referred to as data wrangling.

Feature extraction and pipeline

Once your features and datasets have been obtained, the next step is to perform feature extraction. Feature extraction, depending on the size of your dataset and your features, could be one of the most time-consuming elements of the model building process.

For example, let's say that the results from the aforementioned fictitious John Doe County Election Poll had 40,000 responses. Each response was stored in a SQL database captured from a web form. Performing a SQL query, let's say you then returned all of the data into a CSV file, using which your model can be trained. At a high level, this is your feature extraction and pipeline. For more complex scenarios, such as predicting malicious web content or image classification, the extraction will include binary extraction of specific bytes in files. Properly storing this data to avoid having to re-run the extraction is crucial to iterating quickly (assuming the features did not change).

In Chapter 11, *Training and Building Production Models*, we will deep dive into ways to version your feature-extracted data and maintain control over your data, especially as your dataset grows in size.

Model training

After feature extraction, you are now prepared to train your model. Model training with ML.NET, thankfully, is very straightforward. Depending on the amount of data extracted in the feature extraction phase, the complexity of the pipeline, and the specifications of the host machine, this step could take several hours to complete. When your pipeline becomes much larger and your model becomes more complex, you may find yourself requiring potentially more compute resources than your laptop or desktop can provide; tooling such as Spark exists to help you scale to *n* number of nodes.

In Chapter 11, *Training and Building Production Models*, we will discuss tooling and tips for scaling this step using an easy-to-use open source project.

Model evaluation

Once the model is trained, the last step is to evaluate the model. The typical approach to model evaluation is to *hold out* a portion of your dataset for evaluation. The idea behind this is to take known data, submit it to your trained model, and measure the efficacy of your model. The critical part of this step is to hold out a representative dataset of your data. If your holdout set is swayed one way or the other, then you will more than likely get a false sense of either high performance or low performance. In the next chapter, we will deep dive into the various scoring and evaluation metrics. ML.NET provides a relatively easy interface to evaluate a model; however, each algorithm has unique properties to verify, which we will review as we deep dive into the various algorithms.

Exploring types of learning

Now that you understand the steps that make up the model building process, the next major component to introduce is the two main types of learning. There are several other types of machine learning, such as reinforcement learning. However, for the scope of this book, we will focus on the two types used for the algorithms ML.NET provides—supervised learning and unsupervised learning. If you are curious about the other types of learning, check out *Machine Learning Algorithms*, Giuseppe Bonaccorso, Packt Publishing.

Supervised learning

Supervised learning is the more common of the two types, and, as such, it is also used for most of the algorithms we will cover in this book. Simply put, supervised learning entails you, as the data scientist, passing the known outputs as part of the training to the model. Take, for instance, the election example discussed earlier in this chapter. With supervised learning, every data point in the election polls that is used as a feature along with whom they say will vote for, are sent to the model during training. This step is traditionally called **labeling** in classification algorithms, in which the output values will be one of the pre-training labels.

Unsupervised learning

Conversely, in unsupervised learning, the typical use case is when figuring out the input and output labels proves to be difficult. Using the election scenario, when you are unsure of what features are really going to provide data points for the model to determine a voter's vote, unsupervised learning could provide value and insight. The benefit of this approach is that the algorithm of your choice determines what features drive your labeling. For instance, using a clustering algorithm such as k-means, you could submit all of the voter data points to the model. The algorithm would then be able to group voter data into clusters and predict unseen data. We will deep dive into unsupervised learning with clustering in Chapter 5, *Clustering Model*.

Exploring various machine learning algorithms

At the heart of machine learning are the various algorithms used to solve complex problems. As mentioned in the introduction, this book will cover five algorithms:

- Binary classification
- Regression
- Anomaly detection
- Clustering
- Matrix factorization

Each will be the focus of a chapter later in the book, but for now, let's get a quick overview of them.

Binary classification

One of the easiest algorithms to understand is binary classification. Binary classification is a supervised machine learning algorithm. As the name implies, the output of a model trained with a binary classification algorithm will return a true or false conviction (as in 0 or 1). Problems best suited to a binary classification model include determining whether a comment is hateful or whether a file is malicious. ML.NET provides several binary classification model algorithms, which we will cover in Chapter 4, *Classification Model*, along with a working example of determining whether a file is malicious or not.

Regression

Another powerful yet easy-to-understand algorithm is regression. Regression is another supervised machine learning algorithm. Regression algorithms return a real value as opposed to a binary algorithm or ones that return from a set of specific values. You can think of regression algorithms as an algebra equation solver where there are a number of known values and the goal is to predict the one unknown value. Some examples of problems best suited to regression algorithms are predicting attrition, weather forecasting, stock market predictions, and house pricing, to name a few.

In addition, there is a subset of regression algorithms called **logistic regression** models. Whereas a traditional linear regression algorithm, as described earlier, returns the predicted value, a logistic regression model will return the probability of the outcome occurring.

ML.NET provides several regression model algorithms, which we will cover in Chapter 3, *Regression Model*.

Anomaly detection

Anomaly detection, as the name implies, looks for unexpected events in the data submitted to the model. Data for this algorithm, as you can probably guess, requires data over a period of time. Anomaly detection in ML.NET looks at both spikes and change points. **Spikes**, as the name implies, are temporary, whereas **change points** are the starting points of a longer change.

ML.NET provides an anomaly detection algorithm, which we will cover in Chapter 6, *Anomaly Detection Model*.

Clustering

Clustering algorithms are unsupervised algorithms and offer a unique solution to problems where finding the closest match to related items is the desired solution. During the training of the data, the data is grouped based on the features, and then during the prediction, the closest match is chosen. Some examples of the use of clustering algorithms include file type classification and predicting customer choices.

ML.NET uses the k-means algorithm specifically, which we will deep dive into in Chapter 5, *Clustering Model*.

Matrix factorization

Last but not least, the matrix factorization algorithm provides a powerful and easy-to-use algorithm for providing recommendations. This algorithm is tailored to problems where historical data is available and the problem to solve is predicting a selection from that data, such as movie or music predictions. Netflix's movie suggestion system uses a form of matrix factorization for its suggestions about what movies it thinks you will enjoy.

We will cover matrix factorization in detail in Chapter 7, *Matrix Factorization Model*.

What is ML.NET?

Now that you have a fairly firm understanding of the core machine learning concepts, we can now dive into Microsoft's ML.NET framework. ML.NET is Microsoft's premier machine learning framework. It provides an easy-to-use framework to train, create, and run models with relative ease all in the confines of the .NET ecosystem.

Microsoft's ML.NET was announced and released (version 0.1) in May 2018 at Microsoft's developer conference BUILD in Seattle, Washington. The project itself is open source with an MIT License on GitHub (`https://github.com/dotnet/machinelearning`) and has seen a total of 17 updates since the first release at the time of writing.

Some products using ML.NET internally at Microsoft include Chart Decisions in Excel, Slide Designs in PowerPoint, Windows Hello, and Azure Machine Learning. This emphasizes the production-readiness of ML.NET for your own production deployments.

ML.NET, from the outset, was designed and built to facilitate the use of machine learning for C# and F# developers using an architecture that would come naturally to someone familiar with .NET Framework. Until ML.NET arrived, there was not a full-fledged and supported framework where you could not only train but also run a model without leaving the .NET ecosystem. Google's TensorFlow, for instance, has an open-source wrapper written by Miguel de Icaza available on GitHub (`https://github.com/migueldeicaza/TensorFlowSharp`); however, at the time of writing this book, most workflows require the use of Python to train a model, which can then be consumed by a C# wrapper to run a prediction.

In addition, Microsoft was intent on supporting all of the major platforms .NET developers have grown accustomed to publishing their applications in the last several years. Here are some examples of a few of the platforms, with the frameworks they targeted in parentheses:

- Web (ASP.NET)
- Mobile (Xamarin)
- Desktop (UWP, WPF, and WinForms)
- Gaming (MonoGame and SharpDX)
- IoT (.NET Core and UWP)

Later in this book, we will implement several real-world applications on most of these platforms to demonstrate how to integrate ML.NET into various application types and platforms.

Technical details of ML.NET

With the release of ML.NET 1.4, the targeting of .NET Core 3.0 or later is recommended to take advantage of the hardware intrinsics added as part of .NET Core 3.0. For those unfamiliar, .NET Core 2.x (and earlier) along with .NET Framework are optimized for CPUs with **Streaming SIMD Extensions** (SSE). Effectively, these instructions provide an optimized path for performing several CPU instructions on a dataset. This approach is referred to as **Single Instruction Multiple Data** (SIMD). Given that the SSE CPU extensions were first added in the Pentium III back in 1999 and later added by AMD in the Athlon XP in 2001, this has provided an extremely backward-compatible path. However, this also does not allow code to take advantage of all the advancements made in CPU extensions made in the last 20 years. One such advancement is the **Advanced Vector Extensions** (AVX) available on most Intel and AMD CPUs created in 2011 or later.

This provides eight 32-bit operations in a single instruction, compared to the four SSE provides. As you can probably guess, machine learning can take advantage of this doubling of instructions. For CPUs in .NET Core 3 that are not supported yet (such as ARM), .NET Core 3 automatically falls back to a software-based implementation.

Components of ML.NET

As mentioned previously, ML.NET was designed to be intuitive for experienced .NET developers. The architecture and components are very similar to the patterns found in ASP.NET and WPF.

At the heart of ML.NET is the MLContext object. Similar to AppContext in a .NET application, MLContext is a singleton class. The MLContext object itself provides access to all of the trainer catalogs ML.NET offers (some are offered by additional NuGet packages). You can think of a trainer catalog in ML.NET as a specific algorithm such as binary classification or clustering.

Here are some of the ML.NET catalogs:

- Anomaly detection
- Binary classification
- Clustering
- Forecasting
- Regression
- Time series

These six groups of algorithms were reviewed earlier in this chapter and will be covered in more detail in subsequent dedicated chapters in this book.

In addition, added recently in ML.NET 1.4 was the ability to import data directly from a database. This feature, while in preview at the time of writing, can facilitate not only an easier feature extraction process, but also expands the possibilities of making real-time predictions in an existing application or pipeline possible. All major databases are supported, including SQL Server, Oracle, SQLite, PostgreSQL, MySQL, DB2, and Azure SQL. We will explore this feature in Chapter 4, *Classification Model*, with a console application using a SQLite database.

The following diagram presents the high-level architecture of ML.NET:

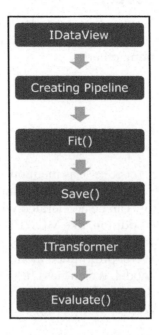

Here, you can see an almost exact match to the traditional machine learning process. This was intentionally done to reduce the learning curve for those familiar with other frameworks. Each step in the architecture can be summarized as follows:

1. **IDataView**: This is used to store the loaded training data into memory.
2. **Creating a Pipeline**: The pipeline creation maps the `IDataView` object properties to values to send to the model for training.
3. **Fit()**: Regardless of the algorithm, after the pipeline has been created, calling `Fit()` kicks off the actual model training.
4. **Save()**: As the name implies, this saves the model (in a binary format) to a file.
5. **ITransformer**: This loads the model back into memory to run predictions.
6. **Evaluate()**: As the name implies, this evaluates the model (`Chapter 2`, *Setting Up the ML.NET Environment* will dive further into the evaluation architecture).

Over the course of this book, we will dive into these methods more thoroughly.

Extensibility of ML.NET

Lastly, ML.NET, like most robust frameworks, provides considerable extensibility. Microsoft has since launched added extensibility support to be able to run the following externally trained model types, among others:

- TensorFlow
- ONNX
- Infer.Net
- CNTK

TensorFlow (`https://www.tensorflow.org/`), as mentioned previously, is Google's machine learning framework with officially supported bindings for C++, Go, Java, and JavaScript. Additionally, TensorFlow can be accelerated with GPUs and, as previously mentioned, Google's own TPUs. In addition, like ML.NET, it offers the ability to run predictions on a wide variety of platforms, including iOS, Android, macOS, ARM, Linux, and Windows. Google provides several pre-trained models. One of the more popular models is the image classification model, which classifies objects in a submitted image. Recent improvements in ML.NET have enabled you to create your own image classifier based on that pre-trained model. We will be covering this scenario in detail in Chapter 12, *Using TensorFlow with ML.NET*.

ONNX (`https://onnx.ai/`), an acronym for Open Neural Network Exchange Format, is a widely used format in the data science field due to the ability to export to a common format. ONNX has converters for XGBoost, TensorFlow, scikit-learn, LibSVM, and CoreML, to name a few. Microsoft's native support of the ONNX format in ML.NET will not only allow better extensibility with existing machine learning pipelines but also increase the adoption of ML.NET in the machine learning world. We will utilize a pre-trained ONNX format model in Chapter 13, *Using ONNX with ML.NET*.

Infer.Net is another open source Microsoft machine learning framework that focuses on probabilistic programming. You might be wondering what probabilistic programming is. At a high level, probabilistic programming handles the grey area where traditional variable types are definite, such as Booleans or integers. Probabilistic programming uses random variables that have a range of values that the result could be, akin to an array. The difference between a regular array and the variables in probabilistic programming is that for every value, there is a probability that the specific value would occur.

A great real-world use of Infer.Net is the technology behind Microsoft's TrueSkill. TrueSkill is a rating system that powers the matchmaking in *Halo* and *Gears of War*, where players are matched based on a multitude of variables, play types, and also, maps can all be attributed to how even two players are. While outside the scope of this book, a great whitepaper diving further into Infer.Net and probabilistic programming, in general, can be found here: `https://dotnet.github.io/infer/InferNet_Intro.pdf`.

CNTK, also from Microsoft, which is short for Cognitive Toolkit, is a deep learning toolkit with a focus on neural networks. One of the unique features of CNTK is its use of describing neural networks via a directed graph. While outside the scope of this book (we will cover neural networks in Chapter 12 with TensorFlow), the world of feed-forward Deep Neural Networks, Convolutional Neural Networks, and Recurrent Neural Networks is extremely fascinating. To dive further into neural networks specifically, I would suggest *Hands-On Neural Network Programming with C#*, also from Packt.

Additional extensibility into Azure and other model support such as PyTorch (`https://pytorch.org/`) is on the roadmap, but no timeline has been established at the time of writing.

Summary

In this chapter, you have learned the importance of discovering machine learning. In addition, you have also learned the core concepts of machine learning, including the differences in learning and the various algorithms we will cover later in this book. You have also received an introduction to ML.NET. The core concepts in this chapter are the foundation for the rest of the book and we will be building on them with each subsequent chapter. In the next chapter, we will be setting up your environment and training your first model in ML.NET!

Setting Up the ML.NET Environment
2

Now that you have a firm grasp of the basics of machine learning, an understanding of what Microsoft's ML.NET is, and what it provides, it is time to train and create your first machine learning model! We will be building a simple restaurant sentiment analysis model based on reviews and integrating this model into a simple .NET Core application. Before we can jump into training and creating our model, we will first have to configure the development environment.

In this chapter, we will cover the following topics:

- Setting up your development environment
- Creating your first model, from start to finish, with ML.NET
- Evaluating the model

Setting up your development environment

Fortunately, configuring your environment for ML.NET is relatively easy. In this section, we will be installing Visual Studio 2019 and .NET Core 3. If you are unsure whether you have either installed, please observe the following steps. In addition, there are some organizational elements and processes to establish early on as we proceed through this book and you begin experimenting on your own.

Installing Visual Studio

At the heart of ML.NET development is Microsoft Visual Studio. For all samples and screenshots used throughout this book, Microsoft Visual Studio 2019 Professional on Windows 10 19H2 will be used. At the time of writing, 16.3.0 is the latest version. Please use the latest version available. If you do not have Visual Studio 2019, a fully featured Community version is available for free on `www.visualstudio.com`.

For the scope of this book as mentioned in `Chapter 1`, *Getting Started with Machine Learning and ML.NET*, we will be creating a wide range of application types to demonstrate ML.NET in various problem areas on specific application platforms. Hence, we are going to install several of the available workloads upfront to avoid having to return to the installer in later chapters:

1. Firstly, ensure that **.NET desktop development**, **Universal Windows Platform Development**, and **ASP.NET and web development** are checked. These workloads will enable you to create UWP, WPF, and ASP.NET applications that we will be using in later chapters:

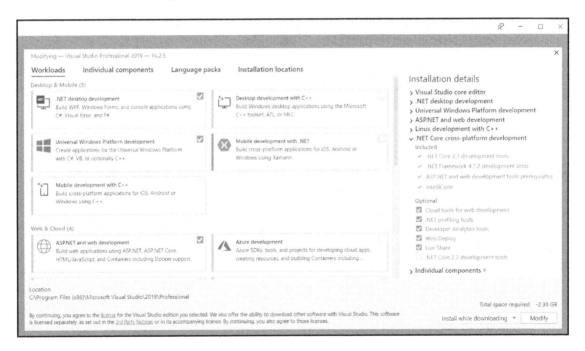

2. In addition, ensure that **.NET Core cross-platform development** is also checked. This will enable .NET Core development for both command-line and desktop apps, such as the app we will be making later in this chapter:

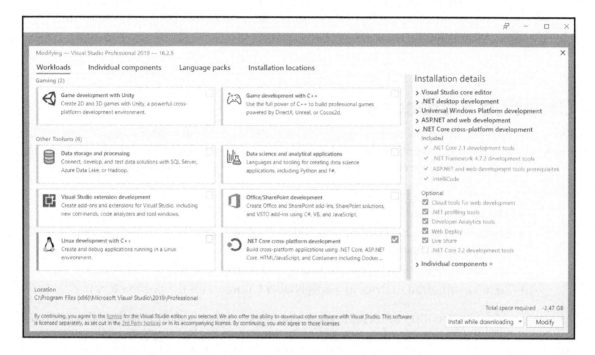

Installing .NET Core 3

As mentioned in `Chapter 1`, *Getting Started with Machine Learning and ML.NET*, .NET Core 3 is the preferred .NET framework at the time of writing when targeting multiple platforms, due to the optimization work achieved during the development of .NET Core 3. At the time of writing .NET Core 3 is not bundled with the Visual Studio Installer prior to version 16.3.0 and needs to be downloaded separately here: `https://dotnet.microsoft.com/download/dotnet-core/3.0`. The download specifically used through the scope of this book is version 3.0.100, but a newer version may be available by the time you are reading this. For those readers who are curious, the runtime is bundled with the SDK.

You can verify that the installation was successful by opening a PowerShell or Command Prompt and executing the following command:

```
dotnet --version
3.0.100
```

The output should begin with 3, as shown here. At the time of writing, 3.0.100 is the latest production version available.

 Be sure to install both 32-bit and 64-bit versions to avoid issues when targeting 32-bit and 64-bit platforms later on in this book and your future experiments.

Creating a process

Over the course of this book and your own explorations, you will gather sample data, build models, and try various applications. Establishing a process early on to keep these elements organized will make things easier in the long run. Here are a few suggestions to keep in mind:

- Always use source control for all of your code.
- Ensure that test and training sets are named properly in their own folders (versioned if possible).
- Versioning models with both naming and source control.
- Retain evaluation metrics in a spreadsheet along with the parameters used.

As you develop your skillset and create more complex problems, additional tooling such as Apache Spark or other clustering platforms will more than likely be required. We will discuss this in Chapter 11, *Training and Building Production Models*, along with other suggestions on training at scale.

Creating your first ML.NET application

The time has come to start creating your first ML.NET application. For this first application, we will create a .NET Core console application. This application will classify a sentence of words as either a positive statement or a negative statement, training on a small sample dataset provided. For this project, we will use a binary logistic regression classification model using the **Stochastic Dual Coordinate Ascent (SDCA)** method. In Chapter 3, *Regression Model*, we will go into greater depth on this method.

Creating the project in Visual Studio

Upon opening, and depending on your configuration in Visual Studio, it will either open directly on to the project creation screen, or will be an empty Visual Studio window. If your environment displays the latter, simply click **File**, then **New**, and then **Project**:

1. When the window opens, type `console app` in the search field to find **Console App (.NET Core)**. Make sure that the language type is C# (there are Visual Basic templates of the same name), highlight this template, and then click **Next**:

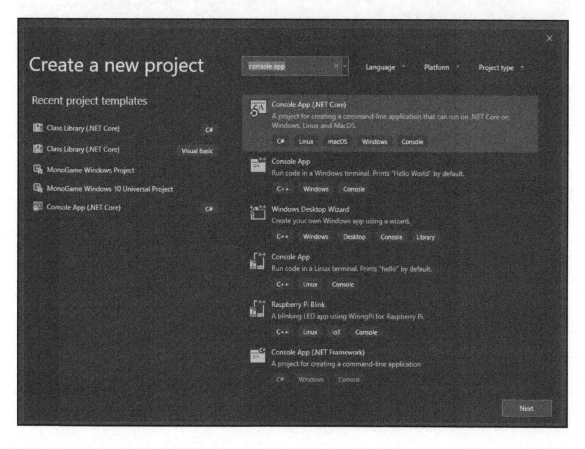

2. I suggest giving the project name something you can refer back to, such as Chapter02, to help you find the project later:

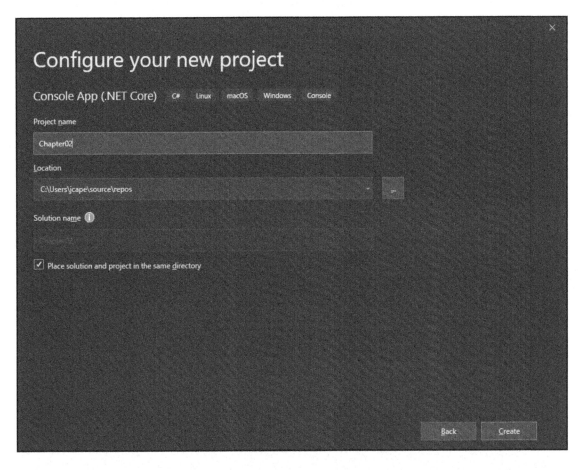

3. At this point, you have a .NET Core 3 console application, so now let's add the ML.NET NuGet package. Right-click on the project and click **Manage NuGet Packages**:

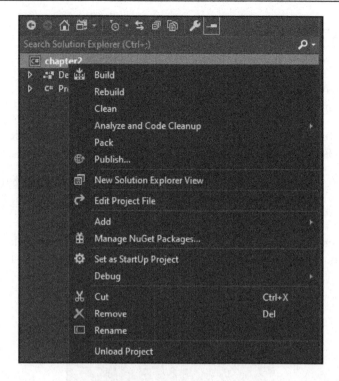

4. Type `microsoft ml` into the search field. You should see the latest `Microsoft.ML` version available:

5. Once found, click the **Install** button. Simple!

 At the time of writing, 1.3.1 is the latest version available and all examples throughout this book will use that version. Prior to 1.0, the syntax was very much in flux, but since then has been consistent, so using a newer version should function identically.

At this point, the project is configured for ML.NET—all future projects will reference ML.NET in this fashion and refer you back to these steps.

Project architecture

The simple project will be split into two primary functions:

- Training and evaluation
- Model runs

This split between functionality models real-world production applications that utilize machine learning, as there are often teams dedicated to each.

For those who wish to start with a completed project and follow along with the rest of this section, you can get the code from here: `https://github.com/PacktPublishing/Hands-On-Machine-Learning-With-ML.NET/tree/master/chapter02`

The following screenshot shows the project breakdown in Solution Explorer of Visual Studio. As mentioned earlier, the project is split into two main classes—`Predictor` and `Trainer`:

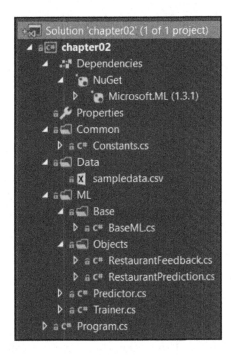

The Trainer class contains all the model building and evaluation code, while the Predictor class, as the name implies, contains the code to run predictions with a trained model.

The BaseML class is what we will be using in subsequent chapters and expanding upon throughout the remainder of the book. The idea behind this class is to cut down on the **DRY (don't repeat yourself)** violations and to create a cohesive and easy to iterate framework. The Constants class further assists this idea—to cut down on magic strings as we move into more complex applications; this design will be used in all future chapter projects.

Lastly, the Program class is the main entry point for our console application.

Running the code

We will now deep dive into the various classes used within this project, including the following classes:

- RestaurantFeedback
- RestaurantPrediction
- Trainer
- Predictor
- BaseML
- Program

The RestaurantFeedback class

The RestaurantFeedback class provides the input class for our model. In ML.NET (and other frameworks), the traditional approach is to have a structured input to feed into your data pipeline, which, in turn, is passed into the training phase and eventually your trained model.

The following class defines our container class to hold our prediction values. This is the approach that we will use throughout the rest of the book:

```
using Microsoft.ML.Data;

namespace chapter02.ML.Objects
{
    public class RestaurantFeedback
```

```
    {
        [LoadColumn(0)]
        public bool Label { get; set; }

        [LoadColumn(1)]
        public string Text { get; set; }
    }
}
```

You might be wondering what the correlation between the Label and Text properties in the RestarauntFeedback class and the source data is at first glance. Contained within the Data folder, there is a file named sampledata.csv. This file contains the following:

```
0    "Great Pizza"
0    "Awesome customer service"
1    "Dirty floors"
1    "Very expensive"
0    "Toppings are good"
1    "Parking is terrible"
0    "Bathrooms are clean"
1    "Management is unhelpful"
0    "Lighting and atmosphere are romantic"
1    "Crust was burnt"
0    "Pineapple was fresh"
1    "Lack of garlic cloves is upsetting"
0    "Good experience, would come back"
0    "Friendly staff"
1    "Rude customer service"
1    "Waiters never came back"
1    "Could not believe the napkins were $10!"
0    "Supersized Pizza is a great deal"
0    "$5 all you can eat deal is good"
1    "Overpriced and was shocked that utensils were an upcharge"
```

The first column maps to the Label property. As you might recall in Chapter 1, *Getting Started with Machine Learning and ML.NET*, supervised learning such as that being performed in this sample requires labeling. In this project, our label is a Boolean. False (0) in the dataset indicates positive feedback, while True (1) indicates negative feedback.

The second column maps to the Text property to propagate the sentiment (which is, the sentence to feed into the model).

The RestaurantPrediction class

The `RestaurantPrediction` class contains the output properties that will come out of our model runs. Depending on the algorithm used, the output class, as you will find in future chapters, will contain many more properties:

```
using Microsoft.ML.Data;

namespace chapter02.ML.Objects
{
    public class RestaurantPrediction
    {
        [ColumnName("PredictedLabel")]
        public bool Prediction { get; set; }

        public float Probability { get; set; }

        public float Score { get; set; }
    }
}
```

Akin to the `RestaurantFeedback Label` property, the `Prediction` property contains the overall result of positive or negative feedback. The `Probability` property contains the confidence of our model of that decision. The `Score` property is used for the evaluation of our model.

The Trainer class

In the following, you will find the sole method in the `Trainer` class. The `Trainer` method at a high level does the following:

- It loads the training data (in this case our CSV) into memory.
- It builds a training set and a test set.
- It creates the pipeline.
- It trains and saves the model.
- It performs an evaluation on the model.

This is the structure and flow we will follow throughout the rest of this book. Now, let's dive into the code behind the `Train` method:

1. First, we check to make sure that the training data filename exists:

```
if (!File.Exists(trainingFileName)) {
    Console.WriteLine($"Failed to find training data file
                      ({trainingFileName}");

    return;
}
```

Even though this is a simple test application, it is always a good practice to treat it like a production-grade application. In addition, since this is a console application, you may incorrectly pass in a path for the training data, which then can cause exceptions further on in the method.

2. Use the `LoadFromTextFile` helper method that ML.NET provides to assist with the loading of text files into an `IDataView` object:

```
IDataView trainingDataView =
       MlContext.Data.LoadFromTextFile<RestaurantFeedback>
       (trainingFileName);
```

As you can see, we are passing in both the training filename and the type; in this case, it is the `RestaurantFeedback` class mentioned earlier. It should be noted that this method has several other parameters, including the following:

- `separatorChar`: This is the column separator character; it defaults to `\t` (in other words, a tab).
- `hasHeader`: If set to `true`, the dataset's first row has the header; it defaults to `false`.
- `allowQuoting`: This defines whether the source file can contain columns defined by a quoted string; it defaults to false.
- `trimWhitespace`: This removes trailing whitespace from the rows; it defaults to false.
- `allowSparse`: This defines whether the file can contain numerical vectors in sparse format; it defaults to false. The sparse format requires a new column to have the number of features.

For most projects used throughout this book, we will use the default settings.

3. Given the `IDataView` object we created previously, use the `TrainTestSplit` method that ML.NET provides to create a test set from the main training data:

```
DataOperationsCatalog.TrainTestData dataSplit =
MlContext.Data.TrainTestSplit(trainingDataView, testFraction: 0.2);
```

As mentioned in Chapter 1, *Getting Started with Machine Learning and ML.NET*, sample data is split into two sets—training and test. The parameter, `testFraction`, specifies the percentage of the dataset to hold back for testing, in our case, 20%. By default, this parameter is set to 0.2.

4. Firstly, we create the pipeline:

```
TextFeaturizingEstimator dataProcessPipeline =
    MlContext.Transforms.Text.FeaturizeText(
        outputColumnName: "Features",
        inputColumnName: nameof(RestaurantFeedback.Text));
```

Future examples will have a much more complex pipeline. In this example, we are simply mapping the `Text` property discussed earlier to the `Features` output column.

5. Next, we instantiate our `Trainer` class:

```
SdcaLogisticRegressionBinaryTrainer sdcaRegressionTrainer =
    MlContext.BinaryClassification.Trainers.SdcaLogisticRegression(
        labelColumnName: nameof(RestaurantFeedback.Label),
        featureColumnName: "Features");
```

As you might remember from Chapter 1, *Getting Started with Machine Learning and ML.NET*, the various algorithms found in ML.NET are referred to as trainers. In this project, we are using an SCDA trainer.

6. Then, we complete the pipeline by appending the trainer we instantiated previously:

```
EstimatorChain<BinaryPredictionTransformer<CalibratedModelParameter
sBase<LinearBinaryModelParameters, PlattCalibrator>>>
trainingPipeline =
dataProcessPipeline.Append(sdcaRegressionTrainer);
```

7. Next, we train the model with the dataset we created earlier in the chapter:

```
ITransformer trainedModel =
trainingPipeline.Fit(dataSplit.TrainSet);
```

8. We save our newly created model to the filename specified, matching the training set's schema:

```
MlContext.Model.Save(trainedModel, dataSplit.TrainSet.Schema,
ModelPath);
```

9. Now, we transform our newly created model with the test set we created earlier:

```
IDataView testSetTransform =
trainedModel.Transform(dataSplit.TestSet);
```

10. Finally, we will use the `testSetTransform` function created previously and pass it into the `BinaryClassification` class's `Evaluate` method:

```
CalibratedBinaryClassificationMetrics modelMetrics =
    MlContext.BinaryClassification.Evaluate(
        data: testSetTransform,
        labelColumnName: nameof(RestaurantFeedback.Label),
        scoreColumnName: nameof(RestaurantPrediction.Score));

Console.WriteLine(
    $"Area Under Curve: {modelMetrics.AreaUnderRocCurve:P2}
        {Environment.NewLine}" +
    $"Area Under Precision Recall Curve:
        {modelMetrics.AreaUnderPrecisionRecallCurve:P2}" +
    $"{Environment.NewLine}" +
    $"Accuracy:
        {modelMetrics.Accuracy:P2}{Environment.NewLine}" +
    $"F1Score:
        {modelMetrics.F1Score:P2}{Environment.NewLine}" +
    $"Positive Recall:
        {modelMetrics.PositiveRecall:#.##}{Environment.NewLine}" +
    $"Negative Recall:
        {modelMetrics.NegativeRecall:#.##}{Environment.NewLine}");
```

This method allows us to generate model metrics. We then print the main metrics using the trained model with the test set. We will dive into these properties specifically in the *Evaluating the Model* section of this chapter.

The Predictor class

The `Predictor` class, as noted earlier, is the class that provides prediction support in our project. The idea behind this method is to provide a simple interface to run the model, given the relatively simple input. In future chapters, we will be expanding this method structure to support more complex integrations, such as those hosted in a web application:

1. Akin to what was done in the `Trainer` class, we verify that the model exists prior to reading it:

```
if (!File.Exists(ModelPath)) {
    Console.WriteLine($"Failed to find model at {ModelPath}");

    return;
}
```

2. Then, we define the `ITransformer` object:

```
ITransformer mlModel;

using (var stream = new FileStream(ModelPath, FileMode.Open,
FileAccess.Read, FileShare.Read))
{
    mlModel = MlContext.Model.Load(stream, out _);
}

if (mlModel == null)
{
    Console.WriteLine("Failed to load model");

    return;
}
```

This object will contain our model once we load via the `Model.Load` method. This method can also take a direct file path. However, the stream approach lends itself to support non on-disk approaches that we will use in later chapters.

3. Next, create a `PredictionEngine` object given the model we loaded earlier:

```
var predictionEngine =
    MlContext.Model.CreatePredictionEngine<RestaurantFeedback,
    RestaurantPrediction>(mlModel);
```

We are passing in both TSrc and TDst, in our case for this project, `RestaurantFeedback` and `RestaurantPrediction`, respectively.

4. Then, call the `Predict` method on the `PredictionEngine` class:

```
var prediction = predictionEngine.Predict(new RestaurantFeedback {
Text = inputData });
```

Because, when we created the object with TSrc, the type was set to `RestaurantFeedback`, we have a strongly typed interface to our model. We then create the `RestaurantFeedback` object with the `inputData` variable that contains the string with the sentence we are going to run our model on.

5. Finally, display the prediction output along with the probability:

```
Console.WriteLine($"Based on \"{inputData}\",
        the feedback is predicted to be:{Environment.NewLine}" +
    "{(prediction.Prediction ? "Negative" : "Positive")}
        at a {prediction.Probability:P0}" + "confidence");
```

The BaseML class

The `BaseML` class, as discussed earlier, is going to contain the common code between our `Trainer` and `Predictor` classes, starting with this chapter. Over the remainder of the book, we will build on top of the `BaseML` class defined as follows:

```
using System;
using System.IO;

using chapter02.Common;

using Microsoft.ML;

namespace chapter02.ML.Base
{
    public class BaseML
    {
        protected static string ModelPath =>
                            Path.Combine(AppContext.BaseDirectory,
                            Constants.MODEL_FILENAME);

        protected readonly MLContext MlContext;

        protected BaseML()
        {
            MlContext = new MLContext(2020);
        }
    }
}
```

For all ML.NET applications in both training and predictions, an `MLContext` object is required. Initializing the object with a specific seed value is needed to create more consistent results during the testing component. Once a model is loaded, the seed value (or lack thereof) does not affect the output.

The Program class

Those of you who have created console applications should be familiar with the `Program` class and the `Main` method within. We will follow this structure for other console-based applications throughout the remainder of the book. The following code block contains the program class from which the application will begin execution:

```
using System;

using chapter02.ML;

namespace chapter02
{
    class Program
    {
        static void Main(string[] args)
        {
            if (args.Length != 2)
            {
                Console.WriteLine(
                    $"Invalid arguments passed in,
                        exiting.{Environment.NewLine}" +
                    $"{Environment.NewLine}Usage: {Environment.NewLine}" +
                    $"predict <sentence of text to predict against>
                        {Environment.NewLine}" +
                    $"or {Environment.NewLine}" +
                    $"train <path to training data file>
                        {Environment.NewLine}");

                return;
            }

            switch (args[0])
            {
                case "predict":
                    new Predictor().Predict(args[1]);
                    break;
                case "train":
                    new Trainer().Train(args[1]);
                    break;
                default:
```

```
                    Console.WriteLine($"{args[0]} is an invalid option");
                    break;
                }
            }
        }
    }
}
```

This constitutes a fairly straightforward method implementation for those familiar with parsing command-line arguments. A simple two-argument approach is used as the help text indicates.

 When executing a more complex command-line application that takes in several arguments (optional and required), Microsoft has provided a simple-to-use NuGet package, which is available here: `https://github.com/dotnet/command-line-api`

Running the example

To run both the training and prediction, simply build the project and then pass in the appropriate data.

For training, you can use the included `sampledata.csv` file or create your own. We will do this by opening a PowerShell window and passing in the relative path:

```
.\chapter02.exe train ..\..\..\Data\sampledata.csv
Area Under Curve: 100.00%
Area Under Precision Recall Curve: 100.00%
Accuracy: 100.00%
F1Score: 100.00%
Positive Recall: 1
Negative Recall: 1
```

Once the model is built, you can run the prediction as follows:

```
.\chapter02.exe predict "bad"
Based on "bad", the feedback is predicted to be:
Negative at a 64% confidence
```

Feel free to try various phrases to test the efficacy of the model, and congratulations on training your first model!

Evaluating the model

As you saw when running the trainer component of the sample project, there are various elements of model evaluation. For each model type, there are different metrics to look at when analyzing the performance of a model.

In binary classification models like the one found in the example project, the following properties are exposed in `CalibratedBiniaryClassificationMetrics` that we set after calling the `Evaluate` method. However, first, we need to define the four prediction types in a binary classification:

- True negative: Properly classified as negative
- True positive: Properly classified as positive
- False negative: Improperly classified as negative
- False positive: Improperly classified as positive

The first metric to understand is **Accuracy**. As the name implies, accuracy is one of the most commonly used metrics when evaluating a model. This metric is calculated simply as the ratio of correctly classified predictions to total classifications.

The next metric to understand is **Precision**. Precision is defined as the proportion of true results over all the positive results in a model. For example, a precision of 1 means there were no false positives, an ideal scenario. A false positive is classifying something as positive when it should be classified as negative, as mentioned previously. A common example of a false positive is misclassifying a file as malicious when it is actually benign.

The next metric to understand is **Recall**. Recall is the fraction of all correct results returned by the model. For example, a recall of 1 means there were no false negatives, another ideal scenario. A false negative is classifying something as negative when it should have been classified as positive.

The next metric to understand is the **F-score**, which utilizes both precision and recall, producing a weighted average based on the false positives and false negatives. F-scores give another perspective on the performance of the model compared to simply looking at accuracy. The range of values is between 0 and 1, with an ideal value of 1.

Area Under the Curve, also referred to as AUC, is, as the name implies, the area under the curve plotted with true positives on the y-axis and false positives on the x-axis. For classifiers such as the model that we trained earlier in this chapter, as you saw, this returned values of between 0 and 1.

Lastly, **Average Log Loss** and **Training Log Loss** are both used to further explain the performance of the model. The average log loss is effectively expressing the penalty for wrong results in a single number by taking the difference between the true classification and the one the model predicts. Training log loss represents the uncertainty of the model using probability versus the known values. As you train your model, you will look to have a low number (lower numbers are better).

As regards the other model types, we will deep dive into how to evaluate them in their respective chapters, where we will cover regression and clustering metrics.

Summary

Over the course of this chapter, we have set up our development environment and learned about the proper organization of files going forward. We also created our first ML.NET application in addition to training, evaluating, and running predictions against a new model. Lastly, we explored how to evaluate a model and what the various properties mean.

In the next chapter, we will deep dive into logistic regression algorithms.

Section 2: ML.NET Models

2

This section talks about using the various trainers available in ML.NET as of version 1.1. In each chapter, a detailed deep dive into the trainer, math, and how to use it with ML.NET will be conveyed.

This section comprises the following chapters:

- Chapter 3, *Regression Model*
- Chapter 4, *Classification Model*
- Chapter 5, *Clustering Model*
- Chapter 6, *Anomaly Detection Model*
- Chapter 7, *Matrix Factorization Model*

Regression Model

3

With our development environment configured and our first ML.NET application completed, it is now time to dive into regression models. In this chapter, we will dive into the math behind regression models, as well as the various applications of regression models. We will also build two additional ML.NET applications, one utilizing a linear regression model and the other a logistic regression model. The linear regression application will predict employee attrition based on various employee attributes. The logistic regression application will perform basic static file analysis on a file to determine whether it is malicious or benign. Finally, we will explore how to evaluate a regression model with the properties ML.NET exposes in regression models.

In this chapter, we will cover the following topics:

- Breaking down various regression models
- Creating the linear regression application
- Creating the logistic regression application
- Evaluating a regression model

Breaking down regression models

While there are several regression model types available in the machine learning ecosystem, there are two primary regression models groups: linear and logistic, both of which have rich implementations in ML.NET.

ML.NET provides the following linear regression trainers:

- `FastTreeRegressionTrainer`
- `FastTreeTweedieTrainer`
- `FastForestRegressionTrainer`
- `GamRegressionTrainer`

- LbfgsPoissonRegressionTrainer
- LightGbmRegressionTrainer
- OlsTrainer
- OnlineGradientDescentTrainer
- SdcaRegressionTrainer

The employee attrition application we will be creating later in this chapter utilizes the linear regression SDCA trainer.

In addition, ML.NET provides the following binary logistic regression trainers:

- LbfgsLogisticRegressionBinaryTrainer
- SdcaLogisticRegressionBinaryTrainer
- SdcaNonCalibratedBinaryTrainer
- SymbolicSgdLogisticRegressionBinaryTrainer

For the file classification application, we will be utilizing the SDCALogisticRegressionBinaryTrainer model.

Choosing the type of regression model

With all of these options, how do you choose the right type of regression model?

The type of regression model you choose depends on what your expected output is. If you are looking for just a Boolean (that is, 0 or 1) value, logistic regression models should be used like in the file classification application we will be writing later in this chapter. In addition, if you are looking to return a specific pre-defined range of values, perhaps a car type such as coupe, convertible, or hatchback, a logistic regression model is the correct model to choose from.

Conversely, linear regression models return a numeric value, such as the employment duration example we will explore later in this chapter.

So, to summarize, we have the following:

- If
  - your output is a Boolean value, use a logistic regression model.
  - If your output is comprised of a preset range type of values (akin to an enumeration), use a logistic regression model.
  - If your output is a numeric unknown value, use a linear regression model.

Choosing a linear regression trainer

When looking at the list of nine linear regression trainers ML.NET, it can be a bit daunting to ask which is the best.

For ML.NET linear regression trainers, by and large, the most popular are FastTree and LightGBM. The three FastTree algorithms utilize neighbor-joining and use heuristics to quickly identify candidate joins to build out a decision tree. LightGBM is a very popular linear regression algorithm that utilizes a **Gradient-based One Side Sampling** (**GOSS**) to filter out the data instances for finding a split value. Both trainers provide both quick training and predict times while also providing very accurate model performance. Also, more documentation, papers, and research are available with both of these algorithms.

 The remaining five trainers are useful and worth a deep dive for experimentation, but overall you will likely find equal or greater success with LightGBM and FastTree.

Choosing a logistic regression trainer

Given the four logistic regression trainers available in ML.NET, which is the best for your problem? Whilst all four regression trainers return a binary classification, they are optimized for different datasets and workloads.

Are you looking to train and predict in a low memory environment? If so, the L-BFGS logistic regression trainer (LbfgsLogisticRegressionBinaryTrainer) is a logical choice given that it was created to handle memory-restricted environments.

Both of the SDCA-based trainers—SdcaLogisticRegressionBinaryTrainer and SdcaNonCalibratedBinaryTrainer—have been optimized for scalability in training. If your training set is large and you are looking for binary classification, either of the SDCA trainers would be a good choice.

The SymbolicSgdLogisticRegressionBinaryTrainer model is different from the other three in that it is based on a stochastic gradient descent algorithm. This means rather than looking to maximize the error function, the algorithm looks to minimize the error function.

If you are curious to expand your knowledge of SCDAs and in particular how Microsoft Research experimented with scaling SCDAs, give this white paper a read: `https://www.microsoft.com/en-us/research/wp-content/uploads/2016/06/main-3.pdf`.

Creating the linear regression application

As mentioned earlier, the application we will be creating is an employee attrition predictor. Given a set of attributes tied to an employee, we can predict how long they will remain at their current job. The attributes included in this example aren't a definitive list of attributes, nor should be used as-is in a production environment; however, we can use this as a starting point for predicting a singular numeric output based on several attributes.

 As with `Chapter 1`, *Getting Started with Machine Learning and ML.NET*, the completed project code, sample dataset, and project files can be downloaded here: `https://github.com/PacktPublishing/Hands-On-Machine-Learning-With-ML.NET/tree/master/chapter03_linear_regression`.

Diving into the trainer

As previously mentioned, for this linear regression application, we will be using the SDCA trainer. **SDCA** stands for **Stochastic Dual Coordinate Ascent** and if you may recall, we used the logistic regression version of this trainer in the example in `Chapter 2`, *Setting Up the ML.NET Environment*.

To the average reader, all four words that comprise SDCA might be unknown, so let's break down what each means to give better clarity to what happens when you utilize an SDCA trainer. Starting with *Stochastic*, which, in other words, means unpredictability. And in the case of machine learning, it means attempting to probabilistically predict the error function and feed random samples from your training set into the optimizer. The use of *Dual Coordinate* means two variables are coupled when training the model. As you have probably guessed, this makes the model much more complex but doesn't require any extra work to be utilized. Lastly, *Ascent* refers to maximizing the value of the error function.

Exploring the project architecture

Building on the project architecture and code we created in Chapter 2, *Setting Up the ML.NET Environment*, the major change architecturally in this example is the mechanism for input. Chapter 2, *Setting Up the ML.NET Environment*, used a simple string to provide sentiment analysis via a command-line argument. In this application, there are several properties to pass into the model; therefore, for this application, we are now using a JSON file to contain our input data. With this addition, we are now including the popular Newtonsoft.Json NuGet package (version 12.0.2 is the latest at the time of this writing and what is used in the included sample). If you are building this project from scratch and do not remember how to add a NuGet reference, please refer back to Chapter 2, *Setting Up the ML.NET Environment*.

The following screenshot shows the Visual Studio Solution Explorer view of the project. The new addition to the solution is the ExtensionMethods class file, which we will review in the next section:

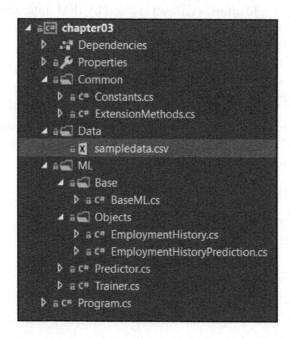

The `sampledata.csv` file contains 40 rows of random data; feel free to adjust the data to fit your own observations or to adjust the trained model. Here is a snippet of the data:

```
16,1,1,0,20,38,1,1,1
23,1,1,1,17,36,0,1,0
6,1,1,0,10,30,1,0,1
4,0,1,0,6,26,1,0,1
14,0,0,0,4,27,1,0,1
24,1,1,1,14,30,1,0,1
5,1,1,0,8,31,0,1,1
12,1,1,0,20,50,0,1,1
12,1,1,0,12,50,1,0,1
6,1,1,0,10,52,0,1,1
```

Each of these rows contains the value for the properties in the newly created `EmploymentHistory` class that we will review later on in this chapter.

 If you want to use a larger dataset to train and expand this example, the website Kaggle offers a dataset created by IBM data scientists. This dataset is available here: `https://www.kaggle.com/pavansubhasht/ibm-hr-analytics-attrition-dataset`.

Diving into the code

For this application as noted, we are building on top of the work completed in Chapter 2, *Setting Up the ML.NET Environment*. For this deep dive, we are going to focus solely on the code that was changed for this application.

The classes that were changed or added are as follows:

- `ExtensionMethods`
- `EmploymentHistory`
- `EmploymentHistoryPrediction`
- `Predictor`
- `Trainer`
- `Program`

The ExtensionMethods class

This newly added class provides an easy to use an extension method to return all of the properties in a class except the label. If you are unfamiliar with extension methods, these methods provide a very simple syntax to potentially provide complex actions on a single object, like in this case, where we take an arbitrary type and return all of the properties it contains (except for `labelName`):

```
using System;
using System.Linq;

namespace chapter03.Common
{
    public static class ExtensionMethods
    {
        public static string[]
            ToPropertyList<T>(this Type objType, string labelName) =>
            objType.GetProperties().Where(a =>
                                        a.Name !=
                                        labelName).
            Select(a => a.Name).ToArray();
    }
}
```

The EmploymentHistory class

The `EmploymentHistory` class is the container class that contains the data to both predict and train our model. These columns map in order for the sample data reviewed previously. If you begin experimenting with new features and add to this list, ensure you increment the array index appropriately:

```
using Microsoft.ML.Data;

namespace chapter03.ML.Objects
{
    public class EmploymentHistory
    {
        [LoadColumn(0)]
        public float DurationInMonths { get; set; }
        [LoadColumn(1)]
        public float IsMarried { get; set; }

        [LoadColumn(2)]
        public float BSDegree { get; set; }

        [LoadColumn(3)]
```

```
        public float MSDegree { get; set; }

        [LoadColumn(4)]
        public float YearsExperience { get; set; }

        [LoadColumn(5)]
        public float AgeAtHire { get; set; }

        [LoadColumn(6)]
        public float HasKids { get; set; }

        [LoadColumn(7)]
        public float WithinMonthOfVesting { get; set; }

        [LoadColumn(8)]
        public float DeskDecorations { get; set; }

        [LoadColumn(9)]
        public float LongCommute { get; set; }
    }
}
```

The EmploymentHistoryPrediction class

The EmploymentHistoryPrediction class contains only the prediction value of how many months the employee is projected to be at his or her job in the DurationInMonths property:

```
using Microsoft.ML.Data;

namespace chapter03.ML.Objects
{
    public class EmploymentHistoryPrediction
    {
        [ColumnName("Score")]
        public float DurationInMonths;
    }
}
```

The Predictor class

There are a couple of changes in this class to handle the employment prediction scenario:

1. First, validate that the input file exists before making a prediction on it:

```
if (!File.Exists(inputDataFile))
{
    Console.WriteLine($"Failed to find input data at
{inputDataFile}");
    return;
}
```

2. The other change is in the prediction call itself. As you probably guessed, the
   TSrc and TDst arguments need to be adjusted to utilize both of the new classes
   we created, `EmploymentHistory` and `EmploymentHistoryPrediction`:

```
var predictionEngine =
MlContext.Model.CreatePredictionEngine<EmploymentHistory,
EmploymentHistoryPrediction>(mlModel);
```

3. Given that we are no longer simply passing in the string and building an object
   on the fly, we need to first read in the file as text. We then deserialize the JSON
   into our `EmploymentHistory` object:

```
var json = File.ReadAllText(inputDataFile);

var prediction =
predictionEngine.Predict(JsonConvert.DeserializeObject<EmploymentHi
story>(json));
```

4. Lastly, we need to adjust the output of our prediction to match our new
   `EmploymentHistoryPrediction` properties:

```
Console.WriteLine(
            $"Based on input
            json:{System.Environment.NewLine}" +
            $"{json}{System.Environment.NewLine}" +
            $"The employee is predicted to work
            {prediction.DurationInMonths:#.##}  months");
```

The Trainer class

Inside the `Trainer` class, a large portion was rewritten to handle the expanded features used and to provide regression algorithm evaluation as opposed to the binary classification we looked at in Chapter 2, *Setting Up the ML.NET Environment*.

The first change is the use of a comma to separate the data as opposed to the default tab like we used in Chapter 2, *Setting Up the ML.NET Environment*:

```
var trainingDataView =
MlContext.Data.LoadFromTextFile<EmploymentHistory>(trainingFileName, ',');
```

The next change is in the pipeline creation itself. In our first application, we had a label and fed that straight into the pipeline. With this application, we have nine features to predict the duration of a person's employment in the `DurationInMonths` property and append each one of them to the pipeline using the C# 6.0 feature, `nameof`. You might have noticed the use of magic strings to map class properties to features in various code samples on GitHub and MSDN; personally, I find this error-prone compared to the strongly typed approach.

For every property, we call the `NormalizeMeanVariance` transform method, which as the name implies normalizes the input data both on the mean and the variance. ML.NET computes this by subtracting the mean of the input data and dividing that value by the variance of the inputted data. The purpose behind this is to nullify outliers in the input data so the model isn't skewed to handle an edge case compared to the normal range. For example, suppose the sample dataset of employment history had 20 rows and all but one of those rows had a person with 50 years experience. The one row that didn't fit would be normalized to better fit within the ranges of values entered into the model.

In addition, note the use of the extension method referred to earlier to help to simplify the following code, when we concatenate all of the feature columns:

```
var dataProcessPipeline = MlContext.Transforms.CopyColumns("Label",
nameof(EmploymentHistory.DurationInMonths))
    .Append(MlContext.Transforms.NormalizeMeanVariance(nameof
(EmploymentHistory.IsMarried)))
    .Append(MlContext.Transforms.NormalizeMeanVariance(nameof
(EmploymentHistory.BSDegree)))
    .Append(MlContext.Transforms.NormalizeMeanVariance(nameof
(EmploymentHistory.MSDegree)))
    .Append(MlContext.Transforms.NormalizeMeanVariance(nameof
(EmploymentHistory.YearsExperience))
    .Append(MlContext.Transforms.NormalizeMeanVariance(nameof
(EmploymentHistory.AgeAtHire)))
    .Append(MlContext.Transforms.NormalizeMeanVariance(nameof
```

```
(EmploymentHistory.HasKids)))
.Append(MlContext.Transforms.NormalizeMeanVariance(nameof
(EmploymentHistory.WithinMonthOfVesting)))
.Append(MlContext.Transforms.NormalizeMeanVariance(nameof
(EmploymentHistory.DeskDecorations)))
.Append(MlContext.Transforms.NormalizeMeanVariance(nameof
(EmploymentHistory.LongCommute)))
.Append(MlContext.Transforms.Concatenate("Features",
    typeof(EmploymentHistory).ToPropertyList<EmploymentHistory>
    (nameof(EmploymentHistory.DurationInMonths))))));
```

We can then create the `Sdca` trainer using the default parameters (`"Label"` and `"Features"`):

```
var trainer = MlContext.Regression.Trainers.Sdca(labelColumnName:
"Label", featureColumnName: "Features");
```

Lastly, we call the `Regression.Evaluate` method to provide regression specific metrics, followed by a `Console.WriteLine` call to provide these metrics to your console output. We will go into detail about what each of these means in the last section of this chapter:

```
var modelMetrics = MlContext.Regression.Evaluate(testSetTransform);

Console.WriteLine($"Loss Function:
                {modelMetrics.LossFunction:0.##}{Environment.NewLine}" +
                $"Mean Absolute Error:
                {modelMetrics.MeanAbsoluteError:#.##}
                {Environment.NewLine}" +
                $"Mean Squared Error:
                {modelMetrics.MeanSquaredError:#.##}
                {Environment.NewLine}" +
                $"RSquared:
                {modelMetrics.RSquared:0.##}{Environment.NewLine}" +
                $"Root Mean Squared Error:
                {modelMetrics.RootMeanSquaredError:#.##}");
```

The Program class

The only change in the `Program` class was the help text to indicate usage for predict requires a filename, not a string:

```
if (args.Length != 2)
{
    Console.WriteLine($"Invalid arguments passed in,
                    exiting.{Environment.NewLine}{Environment.NewLine}
                    Usage:{Environment.NewLine}" +
```

```
                        $"predict <path to input json file>
                        {Environment.NewLine}" +
                        $"or {Environment.NewLine}" +
                        $"train <path to training data file>
                        {Environment.NewLine}");

        return;
    }
```

Running the application

To run the application the process is nearly identical to Chapter 2's sample application. To iterate more quickly, the debug configuration automatically passes in the included `sampledata.csv` file as a command-line parameter:

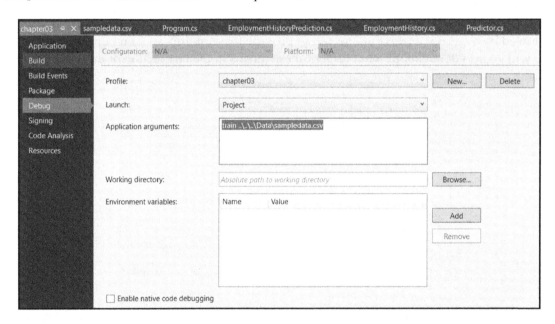

Going forward, due to the increasing complexity of the applications, all sample applications will have this preset:

1. To run the training on the command line as we did in Chapter 1, *Getting Started with Machine Learning and ML.NET,* simply pass in the following command (assuming you are using the included sample dataset):

   ```
   PS chapter03\bin\Debug\netcoreapp3.0> .\chapter03.exe train
   ..\..\..\Data\sampledata.csv
   ```

```
Loss Function: 324.71
Mean Absolute Error: 12.68
Mean Squared Error: 324.71
RSquared: 0.14
Root Mean Squared Error: 18.02
```

Note the expanded output to include several metric data points—we will go through what each one of these means at the end of this chapter.

2. After training the model, build a sample JSON file and save it as `input.json`:

```
{
   "durationInMonths": 0.0,
   "isMarried": 0,
   "bsDegree": 1,
   "msDegree": 1,
   "yearsExperience": 2,
   "ageAtHire": 29,
   "hasKids": 0,
   "withinMonthOfVesting": 0,
   "deskDecorations": 1,
   "longCommute": 1
}
```

3. To run the model with this file, simply pass in the filename to the built application and the predicted output will show:

```
PS chapter03\bin\Debug\netcoreapp3.0> .\chapter03.exe predict
input.json
Based on input json:
{
 "durationInMonths": 0.0,
 "isMarried": 0,
 "bsDegree": 1,
 "msDegree": 1,
 "yearsExperience": 2,
 "ageAtHire": 29,
 "hasKids": 0,
 "withinMonthOfVesting": 0,
 "deskDecorations": 1,
 "longCommute": 1
}

The employee is predicted to work 22.82 months
```

Feel free to modify the values and see how the prediction changes based on the dataset that the model was trained on. A few areas of experimentation from this point might be to do the following:

- Add some additional features based on your own experience.
- Modify `sampledata.csv` to include your team's experience.
- Modify the sample application to have a GUI to make running predicts easier.

Creating the logistic regression application

As mentioned earlier, the application we will be creating to demonstrate logistic regressions is a file classifier. Given a file (of any type), we extract the strings from the file. This is a very common approach to performing file classification although, like the previous example, this is often just an element of file classification, not the only component. Therefore, don't expect this to find the next zero-day piece of malware!

 The completed project code, sample dataset, and project files can be downloaded here: `https://github.com/PacktPublishing/Hands-On-Machine-Learning-With-ML.NET/tree/master/chapter03_logistic_regression`.

The trainer used in this application also uses SDCA but using the logistic regression variation that was discussed earlier in this chapter.

As in the previous example, we will begin by exploring the project architecture, diving into the code, and then show how you can run the example to both train and predict.

Exploring the project architecture

Building on the project architecture and code we created in the previous example, the major change architecturally in this example is feature extraction. With this example, we will add in the `FeatureExtractor` class in addition to creating new input and prediction classes. The reason for this is going back to the idea of keeping things separate and well defined as discussed in Chapter 2, *Setting Up the ML.NET Environment*. For this example application and future applications you may write, they, more than likely, will have input files to convert into rows of data. By having a separate class handle this part of the pipeline, you can encapsulate this functionality cleanly.

The following screenshot shows the Visual Studio Solution Explorer view of the project. The new addition to the solution is the FeatureExtractor class file that we will review in the next section:

The sampledata.csv file contains eight rows of random data. Feel free to adjust the data to fit your own observations or adjust the trained model. Here is the included sample data:

```
False !This program cannot be run in DOS mode.L$ SUVWH\$ UVWAVAWH\$
VWAVHWATAUAVAWHA_AA]A\_l$ VWAVHt
False !This program cannot be run in DOS mode.L$ SUVWH\$
VWAVHUVWAVAWHUVWATAUAVAWHA_AA]A\_]UVWAVAWHU
False !This program cannot be run in DOS
mode.$7ckw7ckw7ckw>jv$ckw7cjwiv6ckwRich7ckw9A98u6A9xx ATAVA
False !This program cannot be run in DOS mode.EventSetInformationmshelp URL
calledLaunchFwLink"mshelp
True !This program cannot be run in DOS mode.Fm;Ld
&~_New_ptrt(M4_Alloc_max"uJIif94H3"j?TjV*?invalid
True <</Length
17268/Type/EmbeddedFile/Filter/FlateDecode/Params<</ModDate(D:2019100301264
1+00'00'/Size
True !This program cannot be run in DOS
mode._New_ptr7(_MaskQAlloc_maxtEqx?$xjinvalid argumC:\Program F
True
__gmon_startN_easy_cKcxa_amxBZNSt8ios_bEe4IeD1Evxxe6naDtqv_Z<4endlIcgLSaQ6a
ppw3d_ResumeCXXABI_1.3%d
```

Each of these rows contains two columns worth of data. The first is the classification, with true being malicious and false being benign. These properties are mapped in the newly created `FileInput` class that we will review later on in this chapter.

Diving into the code

For this application as noted, we are building on top of the work completed earlier within this chapter. Again, for this deep dive, we are going to focus solely on the code that was changed for this application.

Classes that were changed or added are as follows:

- FeatureExtractor
- FileInput
- FilePrediction
- BaseML
- Predictor
- Trainer
- Program

The FeatureExtractor class

This newly added class provides our feature extraction for the given folder of files. Once extraction is complete, the classification and strings data is written out to the `sampledata` file:

```
using System;
using System.IO;

using chapter03_logistic_regression.Common;
using chapter03_logistic_regression.ML.Base;

namespace chapter03_logistic_regression.ML
{
    public class FeatureExtractor : BaseML
    {
        public void Extract(string folderPath)
        {
            var files = Directory.GetFiles(folderPath);

            using (var streamWriter =
```

```
                new StreamWriter(Path.Combine(AppContext.BaseDirectory,
                $"../../../Data/{Constants.SAMPLE_DATA}")))
            {
                foreach (var file in files)
                {
                    var strings = GetStrings(File.ReadAllBytes(file));

                    streamWriter.WriteLine($"{file.ToLower().
                    Contains("malicious")}\t{strings}");
                }
            }

            Console.WriteLine($"Extracted {files.Length} to
            {Constants.SAMPLE_DATA}");
        }
    }
}
```

The FileInput class

The `FileInput` class provides the container for the trained classification and the strings data we extract:

```
using Microsoft.ML.Data;

namespace chapter03_logistic_regression.ML.Objects
{
    public class FileInput
    {
        [LoadColumn(0)]
        public bool Label { get; set; }

        [LoadColumn(1)]
        public string Strings { get; set; }
    }
}
```

The FilePrediction class

The `FilePrediction` class provides the container for the classification, probability, and score:

```
using Microsoft.ML.Data;

namespace chapter03_logistic_regression.ML.Objects
```

```
{
    public class FilePrediction
    {
        [ColumnName("PredictedLabel")]
        public bool IsMalicious { get; set; }

        public float Probability { get; set; }

        public float Score { get; set; }
    }
}
```

The BaseML class

For the `BaseML` class, we have made several enhancements, starting with the constructor. In the constructor, we initialize the `stringRex` variable to the regular expression we will use to extract strings. `Encoding.RegisterProvider` is critical to utilize the Windows-1252 encoding. This encoding is the encoding Windows Executables utilize:

```
private static Regex _stringRex;

protected BaseML()
{
    MlContext = new MLContext(2020);

    Encoding.RegisterProvider(CodePagesEncodingProvider.Instance);

    _stringRex = new Regex(@"[ -~\t]{8,}", RegexOptions.Compiled);
}
```

The next major addition is the `GetStrings` method. This method takes the bytes, runs the previously created compiled regular expression, and extracts the string matches:

1. To begin, we define the method definition and initialize the `stringLines` variable to hold the strings:

   ```
   protected string GetStrings(byte[] data)
   {
       var stringLines = new StringBuilder();
   ```

2. Next, we will sanity check the input data is not null or empty:

   ```
   if (data == null || data.Length == 0)
   {
       return stringLines.ToString();
   }
   ```

3. The next block of code we open a `MemoryStream` object and then a `StreamReader` object:

```
using (var ms = new MemoryStream(data, false))
{
    using (var streamReader = new StreamReader
(ms, Encoding.GetEncoding(1252), false, 2048, false))
    {
```

4. We will then loop through the `streamReader` object until an `EndOfStream` condition is reached, reading line by line:

```
while (!streamReader.EndOfStream)
{
    var line = streamReader.ReadLine();
```

5. We then will apply some string clean up of the data and handle whether the line is empty or not gracefully:

```
if (string.IsNullOrEmpty(line))
{
    continue;
}

line = line.Replace("^", "").Replace(")", "").Replace("-", "");
```

6. Then, we will append the regular expression matches and append those matches to the previously defined `stringLines` variable:

```
stringLines.Append
    (string.Join(string.Empty,
    _stringRex.Matches(line).Where(a => !string.IsNullOrEmpty
                            (a.Value) &&
                            !string.IsNullOrWhiteSpace
                            (a.Value)).ToList()));
```

7. Lastly, we will return the `stringLines` variable converted into a single string using the `string.Join` method:

```
    return string.Join(string.Empty, stringLines);
}
```

The Predictor class

The `Predictor` class, much like what was changed in the linear regression example, is simply modified to support the new model and return the classification:

1. We begin by passing in the two new classes, `FileInput` and `FilePrediction`, to the `CreatePredictionEngine` method:

    ```
    var predictionEngine =
    MlContext.Model.CreatePredictionEngine<FileInput,
    FilePrediction>(mlModel);
    ```

2. Next, we create the `FileInput` object, setting the `Strings` property with the return value of the `GetStrings` method we wrote earlier:

    ```
    var prediction = predictionEngine.Predict(new FileInput
    {
        Strings = GetStrings(File.ReadAllBytes(inputDataFile))
    });
    ```

3. Finally, we update the output call to the `Console` object with our file classification and probability:

    ```
    Console.WriteLine(
                    $"Based on the file ({inputDataFile})
                    the file is classified as
                    {(prediction.IsMalicious ?
                    "malicious" : "benign")}" +
                    $" at a confidence level of
                    {prediction.Probability:P0}");
    ```

The Trainer class

In the `Trainer` class, we will build a new pipeline to train our model. The `FeaturizeText` transform builds NGrams from the strings data we previously extracted from the files. **NGrams** are a popular method to create vectors from a string to, in turn, feed the model. You can think of NGrams as breaking a longer string into ranges of characters based on the value of the NGram parameter. A bi-gram, for instance, would take the following sentence, *ML.NET is great* and convert it into *ML-.N-ET-is-gr-ea-t*. Lastly, we build the `SdcaLogisticRegression` trainer object:

```
var dataProcessPipeline = MlContext.Transforms.CopyColumns("Label",
nameof(FileInput.Label))
    .Append(MlContext.Transforms.Text.FeaturizeText("NGrams",
    nameof(FileInput.Strings)))
```

```
    .Append(MlContext.Transforms.Concatenate("Features",
    "NGrams"));

var trainer =
MlContext.BinaryClassification.Trainers.SdcaLogisticRegression
(labelColumnName: "Label", featureColumnName: "Features");
```

 For those looking to deep dive further into the `Transforms` Catalog API, check out the documentation from Microsoft here: `https://docs.` `microsoft.com/en-us/dotnet/api/microsoft.ml.transformscatalog?` `view=ml-dotnet.`

The Program class

In the `Program` class, we added a third option to extract features and create the sample data `.tsv` file:

1. To begin, we modify the help text to indicate the new extract option that takes a path to the training folder:

```
if (args.Length != 2)
{
    Console.WriteLine($"Invalid arguments passed in,
                      exiting.{Environment.NewLine}
                      {Environment.NewLine}
                      Usage:{Environment.NewLine}" +
                      $"predict <path to input file>
                      {Environment.NewLine}" +
                      $"or {Environment.NewLine}" +
                      $"train <path to training data file>
                      {Environment.NewLine}" +
                      $"or {Environment.NewLine}" +
                      $"extract <path to folder>
                      {Environment.NewLine}");

    return;
}
```

2. In addition, we also need to modify the main switch/case to support the `extract` argument:

```
switch (args[0])
{
    case "extract":
        new FeatureExtractor().Extract(args[1]);
        break;
```

```
case "predict":
    new Predictor().Predict(args[1]);
    break;
case "train":
    new Trainer().Train(args[1]);
    break;
default:
    Console.WriteLine($"{args[0]} is an invalid option");
    break;
}
```

Running the application

With the addition of feature extraction in our pipeline, we first need to perform feature extraction on the files:

1. Assuming the folder of files called `temp_data` exists, execute the following command:

   PS chapter03-logistic-regression\bin\Debug\netcoreapp3.0> .\chapter03-logistic-regression.exe extract temp_data
   Extracted 8 to sampledata.csv

   The output shows the count of extracted files and the output sample file.

2. To train the model using either the included `sampledata.csv` or one you trained yourself, execute the following command:

   PS chapter03-logistic-regression\bin\Debug\netcoreapp3.0> .\chapter03-logistic-regression.exe train ..\..\..\Data\sampledata.csv

   The `chapter3.mdl` model file should exist in the folder executed in once complete.

3. To run the newly trained model against an existing file such as the compiled `chapter3` executable, run the following command:

   PS chapter03-logistic-regression\bin\Debug\netcoreapp3.0> .\chapter03-logistic-regression.exe predict .\chapter03-logistic-regression.exe
   Based on the file (.\chapter03-logistic-regression.exe) the file is classified as benign at a confidence level of 8%

If you are looking for sample files, the `c:\Windows` and `c:\Windows\System32` folders contain numerous Windows Executables and DLLs. In addition, if you are looking to create malicious-looking files that are actually clean, you can create files on the fly on `http://cwg.io` in various file formats. This is a helpful tool in the cyber-security space where testing new functionality on a development machine is much safer than detonating real zero-day threats on!

Evaluating a regression model

As discussed in previous chapters, evaluating a model is a critical part of the overall model building process. A poorly trained model will only provide inaccurate predictions. Fortunately, ML.NET provides many popular attributes to calculate model accuracy based on a test set at the time of training to give you an idea of how well your model will perform in a production environment.

In ML.NET, as noted earlier in the linear regression sample application, there are five properties that comprise the `RegressionMetrics` class object. These include the following:

- Loss function
- Mean absolute error
- Mean squared error
- R-squared
- Root mean squared error

In the next sections, we will break down how these values are calculated and ideal values to look for.

Loss function

This property uses the loss function set when the regression trainer was initialized. In the case of our linear regression example application, we used the default constructor, which for SDCA is defaulted to the `SquaredLoss` class.

Other regression loss functions offered by ML.NET are the following:

- `TweedieLoss` (used for Tweedie regression models)
- `PoissonLoss` (used for Poisson regression models)

The idea behind this property is to allow some flexibility when it comes to evaluating your model compared to the other four properties that use fixed algorithms for evaluation.

Mean squared error

Mean Squared Error, also known as **MSE**, is defined as the measure of the average of the squares of the errors. To put it simply, please refer to the following plot:

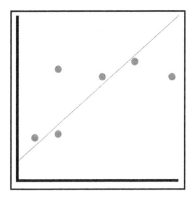

The dots correlate to data points for our model, while the line going across is the prediction line. The distance between the dots and the prediction line is the error. For MSE, the value is calculated based on these points and their distances to the line. From that value, the mean is calculated. For MSE, the smaller the value, the better fitting and more accurate predictions you will have with your model.

MSE is best used to evaluate models when outliers are critical to the prediction output.

Mean absolute error

Mean Absolute Error, also known as **MAE**, is similar to MSE, with the critical difference that it sums the distances between the points and the prediction lines as opposed to computing the mean. It should be noted, MAE does not take into account directions in calculating the sum. For instance, if you had two data points, equidistant from the line, one being above and the other below, in effect, this would be balanced out with a positive and negative value. In machine learning, this is referred to as mean bias error, however, ML.NET does not provide this as part of the `RegressionMetrics` class at the time of this writing.

MAE is best used to evaluate models when outliers are considered simply anomalies and shouldn't be counted in evaluating a model's performance.

R-squared

R-squared, also called the coefficient of determination, is another method of representing how accurate the prediction is compared to the test set. R-squared is calculated by taking the sum of the distance between every data point and the mean squared, subtracting them and then squaring it.

R-squared values generally range between 0 and 1, represented as a floating-point value. A negative value can occur when the fitted model is evaluated to be worse than an average fit. However, a low number does not always reflect that the model is bad. Predictions such as the one we looked at in this chapter that is based on predicting human actions are often found to be under 50%.

Conversely, higher values aren't necessarily a sure sign of the model's performance, as this could be considered an overfitting of the model. This happens in cases when there are a lot of features fed to the model, thereby making the model more complex than, for instance, the model we built in Chapter 1, *Getting Started with Machine Learning and ML.NET*, or there is simply not enough diversity in the training and test sets. For example, if all of the employees were roughly the same values, and the test set holdout was comprised of the same ranges of values, this would be considered overfitting.

Root mean squared error

Root mean squared error, also known as **RMSE**, is arguably the easiest to understand given the previous methods. Take the following plot:

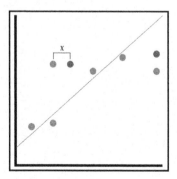

In the case of testing the model as we did previously with the holdout set, the lighter dots are the actual values from the test set, while the darker dots are the predicted values. The X depicted is the distance between the predicted and actual values. RMSE simply takes a mean of all of those distances, squares that value, and then takes the square root.

A value under 180 is generally considered a good model.

Summary

Throughout this chapter, we looked into the differences between linear and logistic regression models. In addition, we reviewed when to choose linear or logistic models along with the trainers ML.NET provides. We also created and trained our first linear regression application using SDCA and ML.NET to predict employee attrition. We also created a logistic regression application using SDCA and ML.NET to provide file classification. Lastly, we also dove into how to evaluate a regression model and the various properties that ML.NET exposes to achieve a proper evaluation of your regression models.

In the next chapter, we will deep dive into binary classification algorithms.

Classification Model

4

With regression models behind us, it is now time to dive into classification models. In this chapter, we will examine the math behind classification models, as well as the various applications of classification models. In addition, we will build two new ML.NET classification applications: the first, a binary classification example that will predict if a car's price is a good deal or not, akin to what you would find on a car purchase website; the other application, a multi-class classification application that categorizes emails. Finally, we will explore how to evaluate a classification model with the properties ML.NET exposes in classification models.

In this chapter, we will cover the following topics:

- Breaking down classification models
- Creating a binary classification application
- Creating a multi-class classification application
- Evaluating a classification model

Breaking down classification models

As mentioned in Chapter 1, *Getting Started with Machine Learning and ML.NET*, classification is broken down into two main categories—two-class and multi-class. In a two-class classifier, also known as a binary classifier, the prediction simply returns 0 or 1. In a multi-class problem, a pre-selected range of return labels, such as virus types or car types, is returned.

There are several binary classification model types available in the machine learning ecosystem to choose from, as follows:

- AveragedPerceptronTrainer
- SdcaLogisticRegressionBinaryTrainer
- SdcaNonCalibratedBinaryTrainer

- `SymbolicSgdLogisticRegressionBinaryTrainer`
- `LbfgsLogisticRegressionBinaryTrainer`
- `LightGbmBinaryTrainer`
- `FastTreeBinaryTrainer`
- `FastForestBinaryTrainer`
- `GamBinaryTrainer`
- `FieldAwareFactorizationMachineTrainer`
- `PriorTrainer`
- `LinearSvmTrainer`

The car-value application we will be creating later in this chapter utilizes the `FastTreeBinaryTrainer` model.

ML.NET also provides the following multi-class classifiers:

- `LightGbmMulticlassTrainer`
- `SdcaMaximumEntropyMulticlassTrainer`
- `SdcaNonCalibratedMulticlassTrainer`
- `LbfgsMaximumEntropyMulticlassTrainer`
- `NaiveBayesMulticlassTrainer`
- `OneVersusAllTrainer`
- `PairwiseCouplingTrainer`

For the multi-class classifier example application, we will be using the `SdcaMaximumEntropyMulticlassTrainer` model. The reason for this is that **Stochastic Dual Coordinate Ascents (SDCAs)** can provide a good default performance without tuning.

Choosing a classification trainer

Given the two types of classification, which should you choose? As stated earlier in this chapter, compared to regression models, your prediction output type will decide between binary and multi-class classification. Does your problem simply predict a value of true or false, or does it provide a more varied output based on a pre-defined value set? If your answer is the former, you need to use a binary classification. If the latter, you will need to use a multi-class classification. In this chapter, we will demonstrate both model prediction types.

For specific binary classification trainers, SDCA, LightGBM, and FastTree are the most popular options, as well as the most documented.

For specific multi-class classification trainers, LightGBM and SDCA are the most popular and best-documented options.

Creating a binary classification application

As mentioned earlier, the application we will be creating is a car-value predictor. Given a set of attributes tied to a car, one can predict if the price is a good deal or not. The attributes included in this example aren't a definitive list of attributes, nor should they be used as-is in a production environment. However, one could use this as a starting point for predicting a simple true-or-false answer based on several attributes.

As with previous chapters, the complete project code, sample dataset, and project files can be downloaded here: https://github.com/PacktPublishing/Hands-On-Machine-Learning-With-ML.NET/tree/master/chapter04.

Diving into the trainer

As previously mentioned, for this binary classification application, we will be using the FastTree trainer.

FastTree is based on the **Multiple Additive Regression Trees (MART)** gradient boosting algorithm. Gradient boosting is a very popular technique, in which a series of trees are built in a step-wise manner before ultimately selecting the best tree. MART takes this approach a step further by learning an ensemble of regression trees that use scalar values in their leaves.

The FastTree trainer doesn't require normalization but does require all of the feature columns to use a `float` variable type and the label column to be a `bool` variable type.

 If you are curious about MART, Cornell University has a paper from 2015 on the subject: https://arxiv.org/abs/1505.01866.

Exploring the project architecture

Building on the project architecture and code we created in Chapter 3, *Regression Model*, the major change architecturally in this example is the mechanism for input. For this application, since we are using the FastTree algorithm, this requires referencing the Microsoft.ML.FastTree NuGet package (version 1.3.1 is the latest at the time of this writing). If you are building this project from scratch and do not remember how to add a NuGet reference, please refer back to Chapter 2, *Setting Up the ML.NET Environment*.

In the following screenshot, you will find the Visual Studio Solution Explorer view of the project. The new addition to the solution is the testdata.csv file, which we will review here:

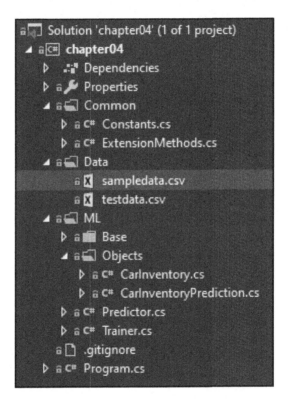

The `sampledata.csv` file contains 18 rows of random data. Feel free to adjust the data to fit your own observations or to adjust the trained model. Here is a snippet of the data:

```
0,0,0,4000,0
1,1,1,4500,1
0,1,0,5000,0
0,0,1,4500,0
0,0,0,3000,1
0,1,0,3100,1
0,1,1,3500,1
1,1,1,5500,0
1,1,1,4200,1
```

Each of these rows contains the value for the properties in the newly created `CarInventory` class that we will review later on in this chapter.

In addition, in this chapter, we added the `testdata.csv` file that contains additional data points to test the newly trained model against and evaluate. Here is a snippet of the data inside of `testdata.csv`:

```
0,0,0,2010,1
1,0,0,2600,1
1,0,0,3700,0
1,1,0,3100,1
1,1,0,3600,0
0,1,0,3500,0
0,0,1,3400,1
0,0,1,5100,0
```

Diving into the code

For this application, as noted in the previous section, we are building on top of the work completed in Chapter 3, *Regression Model*. For this deep dive, we are going to focus solely on the code that was changed for this application.

Classes that were changed or added are as follows:

- `CarInventory`
- `CarInventoryPrediction`
- `Predictor`
- `Trainer`
- `Program`

The CarInventory class

The CarInventory class is the container class that contains the data to both predict and train our model. These columns map in order of the sample data reviewed previously. If you begin experimenting with new features and add to the following class, ensure you increment the array index appropriately, as follows:

```
using Microsoft.ML.Data;

namespace chapter04.ML.Objects
{
    public class CarInventory
    {
        [LoadColumn(0)]
        public float HasSunroof { get; set; }

        [LoadColumn(1)]
        public float HasAC { get; set; }

        [LoadColumn(2)]
        public float HasAutomaticTransmission { get; set; }

        [LoadColumn(3)]
        public float Amount { get; set; }

        [LoadColumn(4)]
        public bool Label { get; set; }
    }
}
```

The CarInventoryPrediction class

The CarInventoryPrediction class contains the properties mapped to our prediction output, in addition to the Score and Probability properties used for model evaluation. The PredictedLabel property contains our classification result, not the label as in previous chapters, as shown in the following code block:

```
namespace chapter04.ML.Objects
{
    public class CarInventoryPrediction
    {
        public bool Label { get; set; }

        public bool PredictedLabel { get; set; }
```

```
        public float Score { get; set; }

        public float Probability { get; set; }
    }
}
```

The Predictor class

There are a couple of changes in this class to handle the employment-prediction scenario, as follows:

1. The first change is in the prediction call itself. As you probably guessed, the `TSrc` and `TDst` arguments need to be adjusted to utilize both of the new classes we created, `CarInventory` and `CarInventoryPrediction`, like this:

    ```
    var predictionEngine =
    MlContext.Model.CreatePredictionEngine<CarInventory,
    CarInventoryPrediction>(mlModel);
    ```

2. Given that we are no longer simply passing in the string and building an object on the fly, we need to first read in the file as text. We then deserialize the JSON into our `CarInventory` object, as follows:

    ```
    var prediction =
    predictionEngine.Predict(JsonConvert.DeserializeObject<CarInventory
    >
    (json));
    ```

3. Lastly, we need to adjust the output of our prediction to match our new `CarInventoryPrediction` properties, like this:

    ```
    Console.WriteLine(
            $"Based on input json:
            {System.Environment.NewLine}" +
            $"{json}{System.Environment.NewLine}" +
            $"The car price is a
            {(prediction.PredictedLabel ? "good" : "bad")} deal,
            with a {prediction.Probability:P0} confidence");
    ```

The Trainer class

Inside the `Trainer` class, several modifications need to be made to support binary classification, as follows:

1. The first change is the check to ensure the test filename exists, shown in the following code block:

```
if (!File.Exists(testFileName))
{
    Console.WriteLine($"Failed to find test data file
                        ({testFileName}");
    return;
}
```

2. We then build the data process pipeline using the `NormalizeMeanVariance` transform method we used in Chapter 3, *Regression Model*, on the inputted values, like this:

```
IEstimator<ITransformer> dataProcessPipeline =
    MlContext.Transforms.Concatenate("Features",
    typeof(CarInventory).ToPropertyList<CarInventory>
    (nameof(CarInventory.Label)))
.Append(MlContext.Transforms.NormalizeMeanVariance(inputColumnName:
"Features", outputColumnName: "FeaturesNormalizedByMeanVar"));
```

3. We can then create the `FastTree` trainer with the label from the `CarInventory` class and the normalized mean variance, as follows:

```
var trainer = MlContext.BinaryClassification.Trainers.FastTree(
    labelColumnName: nameof(CarInventory.Label),
    featureColumnName: "FeaturesNormalizedByMeanVar",
    numberOfLeaves: 2,
    numberOfTrees: 1000,
    minimumExampleCountPerLeaf: 1,
    learningRate: 0.2);
```

Later on, after you have run the application, consider tweaking the number of leaves and the number of trees to see how both the model metrics and your prediction probability percentage change.

4. Lastly, we call the `Regression.Evaluate` method to provide regression-specific metrics, followed by a `Console.WriteLine` call to provide these metrics to your console output. We will go into detail about what each of these means in the last section of the chapter, but for now, the code can be seen here:

```
var trainingPipeline = dataProcessPipeline.Append(trainer);

var trainedModel = trainingPipeline.Fit(trainingDataView);

MlContext.Model.Save(trainedModel, trainingDataView.Schema,
ModelPath);
```

Now, we evaluate the model we just trained, like this:

```
var evaluationPipeline = trainedModel.Append(MlContext.Transforms
 .CalculateFeatureContribution(trainedModel.LastTransformer)
.Fit(dataProcessPipeline.Fit(trainingDataView).Transform(trainingDa
taView)));

var testDataView =
MlContext.Data.LoadFromTextFile<CarInventory>(testFileName, ',',
hasHeader: false);

var testSetTransform = evaluationPipeline.Transform(testDataView);

var modelMetrics = MlContext.BinaryClassification.Evaluate(data:
testSetTransform,
 labelColumnName: nameof(CarInventory.Label),
 scoreColumnName: "Score");
```

Finally, we output all of the classification metrics. We will detail each of these in the next section, but for now, the code can be seen here:

```
Console.WriteLine($"Accuracy: {modelMetrics.Accuracy:P2}");
Console.WriteLine($"Area Under Curve:
{modelMetrics.AreaUnderRocCurve:P2}");
Console.WriteLine($"Area under Precision recall Curve:
{modelMetrics.AreaUnderPrecisionRecallCurve:P2}");
Console.WriteLine($"F1Score: {modelMetrics.F1Score:P2}");
Console.WriteLine($"LogLoss: {modelMetrics.LogLoss:#.##}");
Console.WriteLine($"LogLossReduction:
{modelMetrics.LogLossReduction:#.##}");
Console.WriteLine($"PositivePrecision:
{modelMetrics.PositivePrecision:#.##}");
Console.WriteLine($"PositiveRecall:
{modelMetrics.PositiveRecall:#.##}");
Console.WriteLine($"NegativePrecision:
{modelMetrics.NegativePrecision:#.##}");
```

```
Console.WriteLine($"NegativeRecall:
{modelMetrics.NegativeRecall:P2}");
```

The Program class

The only change in the `Program` class is the help text to indicate usage for the trainer to accept the test file, shown in the following code block:

```
if (args.Length < 2)
{
    Console.WriteLine(
        $"Invalid arguments passed in, exiting.{Environment.NewLine}
          {Environment.NewLine}Usage:{Environment.NewLine}" +
        $"predict <path to input json file>{Environment.NewLine}" +
        $"or {Environment.NewLine}" +
        $"train <path to training data file><path to test data file>
          {Environment.NewLine}");

    return;
}
```

Finally, we modify the `switch`/`case` statement to support the additional parameter to the `Train` method, as follows:

```
switch (args[0])
{
    case "predict":
        new Predictor().Predict(args[1]);
        break;
    case "train":
        new Trainer().Train(args[1], args[2]);
        break;
    default:
        Console.WriteLine($"{args[0]} is an invalid option");
        break;
}
```

Running the application

To run the application, the process is nearly identical to the sample application in Chapter 3, *Regression Model*, with the addition of passing in the test dataset when training, described as follows:

1. To run the training on the command line, as we did in Chapter 1, *Getting Started with Machine Learning and ML.NET*, we simply pass in the following command (assuming you are using the included sample dataset and test dataset):

```
PS chapter04\bin\Debug\netcoreapp3.0> .\chapter04.exe train
..\..\..\Data\sampledata.csv ..\..\..\Data\testdata.csv
Accuracy: 88.89%
Area Under Curve: 100.00%
Area under Precision recall Curve: 100.00%
F1Score: 87.50%
LogLoss: 2.19
LogLossReduction: -1.19
PositivePrecision: 1
PositiveRecall: .78
NegativePrecision: .82
NegativeRecall: 100.00%
```

Note the expanded output to include several metric data points—we will go through what each one of these means at the end of this chapter.

2. After training the model, build a sample JSON file and save it as input.json, as follows:

```
{
    "HasSunroof":0,
    "HasAC":0,
    "HasAutomaticTransmission":0,
    "Amount":1300
}
```

3. To run the model with this file, simply pass in the filename to the built application, and the predicted output will appear, as follows:

```
PS chapter04\bin\Debug\netcoreapp3.0> .\chapter04.exe predict
.\input.json
Based on input json:
{
"HasSunroof":0,"HasAC":0,"HasAutomaticTransmission":0,"Amount":1300
}
The car price is a good deal, with a 100% confidence
```

Feel free to modify the values and see how the prediction changes based on the dataset on which the model was trained. A few areas of experimentation from this point might be as follows:

- Add some additional features based on your own car-buying experiences
- Modify the `sampledata.csv` file to include your own car-buying experiences
- Modify the sample application to have a **graphical user interface (GUI)** to make running predictions easier

Creating a multi-class classification application

As mentioned earlier, we will now create a multi-class classification application, categorizing email into one of three categories:

- Orders
- Spam
- Friend

Flushing out this example for a production application would more than likely include significantly more categories in addition to more features. However, this is a good starting point to demonstrate a multi-class classification use case.

As with other examples, the complete project code, sample dataset, and project files can be downloaded here: `https://github.com/PacktPublishing/Hands-On-Machine-Learning-With-ML.NET/tree/master/chapter04-multiclass`.

Diving into the trainer

As previously mentioned, for this multi-class classification application we will be using the `SdcaMaximumEntropy` trainer.

The `SdcaMaximumEntropy` class, as the name implies, is based on the SDCA we deep dove into in `Chapter 3`, *Regression Model*, and uses empirical risk minimization, which optimizes based on the training data. This does leave a potential for outliers or anomalies to greatly affect the predict performance. Therefore, when using this trainer, provide the trainer with ample sampling of expected data, to avoid both overfitting and potential errors when predicting data.

The `SdcaMaximumEntropy` trainer, unlike the previous binary classification example, does require normalization. In addition, caching is not required; however, we do utilize caching when building the pipeline.

Exploring the project architecture

Building on the project architecture and code created earlier in this chapter, there are no new NuGet packages to include in this project, as SDCA trainers are considered core trainers. The major change is in the `Training` pipeline, which we will go into in further detail later on in this section.

In the following screenshot, you will find the Visual Studio Solution Explorer view of the project:

The `sampledata.csv` file contains six rows of random data. Feel free to adjust the data to fit your own observations or to adjust the trained model. Here is a snippet of the data:

```
"Order #1234", "Thank you for ordering a new CPU", "order@cpulandia.com",
"orders"
"Get Free Free", "Click here for everything free", "freefree@asasdasd.com",
"spam"
"Checking in", "How is it going?", "johndough@gmail.com", "friend"
"Order 4444", "Thank you for ordering a pizza", "order@pizzalandia.com",
"orders"
"Unlock Free", "Click here to unlock your spam", "spammer@asasdasd.com",
"spam"
"Hello", "Did you see my last message?", "janedough@gmail.com", "friend"
```

Each of these rows contains the value for the properties in the newly created `Email` class that we will review later on in this chapter.

In addition, in this chapter, we added the `testdata.csv` file that contains additional data points to test the newly trained model against. Here is a snippet of the data:

```
"Order 955", "Thank you for ordering a new gpu", "order@gpulandia.com",
"orders"
"Win Free Money", "Lottery winner, click here", "nowfree@asasdasd.com",
"spam"
"Yo", "Hey man?", "john@gmail.com", "friend"
```

Diving into the code

For this application, as noted earlier, we are building on top of the work completed in `Chapter 3`, *Regression Model*. For this deep dive, we are going to focus solely on the code that was changed for this application.

Classes that were changed or added are as follows:

- `Email`
- `EmailPrediction`
- `Predictor`
- `Trainer`
- `Program`

The Email class

The Email class is the container class that contains the data to both predict and train our model. These columns map in order to the sample data reviewed previously. If you begin experimenting with new features and add to this list, ensure you increment the array index appropriately, as shown in the following code block:

```
using Microsoft.ML.Data;

namespace chapter04_multiclass.ML.Objects
{
    public class Email
    {
        [LoadColumn(0)]
        public string Subject { get; set; }

        [LoadColumn(1)]
        public string Body { get; set; }

        [LoadColumn(2)]
        public string Sender { get; set; }

        [LoadColumn(3)]
        public string Category { get; set; }
    }
}
```

The EmailPrediction class

The EmailPrediction class contains the property mapped to our prediction output used for model evaluation. In the following code block, we are returning the Category value (string value):

```
using Microsoft.ML.Data;

namespace chapter04_multiclass.ML.Objects
{
    public class EmalPrediction
    {
        [ColumnName("PredictedLabel")]
        public string Category;
    }
}
```

The Predictor class

There are a couple of changes in this class to handle the email categorization prediction scenario, as follows:

1. The first change is in the prediction call itself. As you probably guessed, the `TSrc` and `TDst` arguments need to be adjusted to utilize both of the new classes we created, `Email` and `EmailPrediction`, as follows:

```
var predictionEngine =
MlContext.Model.CreatePredictionEngine<Email,
EmailPrediction>(mlModel);
```

2. Given that we are no longer simply passing in the string and building an object on the fly, we need to first read in the file as text. We then deserialize the JSON into our `Email` object, like this:

```
var prediction =
predictionEngine.Predict(JsonConvert.DeserializeObject<Email>(json)
);
```

3. Lastly, we need to adjust the output of our prediction to match our new `EmailPrediction` properties, as follows:

```
Console.WriteLine(
    $"Based on input json:{System.Environment.NewLine}" +
    $"{json}{System.Environment.NewLine}" +
    $"The email is predicted to be a {prediction.Category}");
```

The Trainer class

There are a couple of changes in this class to handle the email categorization prediction scenario, as follows:

1. First, we read in the `trainingFileName` string and typecast it to an `Email` object, like this:

```
var trainingDataView =
MlContext.Data.LoadFromTextFile<Email>(trainingFileName, ',',
hasHeader: false);
```

2. Next, we will create our pipeline mapping our input properties to
   `FeaturizeText` transformations before appending our SDCA trainer, as follows:

```
var dataProcessPipeline =
MlContext.Transforms.Conversion.MapValueToKey(inputColumnName:
nameof(Email.Category), outputColumnName: "Label")
.Append(MlContext.Transforms.Text.FeaturizeText(inputColumnName:
nameof(Email.Subject), outputColumnName: "SubjectFeaturized"))
.Append(MlContext.Transforms.Text.FeaturizeText(inputColumnName:
nameof(Email.Body), outputColumnName: "BodyFeaturized"))
.Append(MlContext.Transforms.Text.FeaturizeText(inputColumnName:
nameof(Email.Sender), outputColumnName: "SenderFeaturized"))
    .Append(MlContext.Transforms.Concatenate("Features",
"SubjectFeaturized", "BodyFeaturized", "SenderFeaturized"))
    .AppendCacheCheckpoint(MlContext);

var trainingPipeline = dataProcessPipeline
.Append(MlContext.MulticlassClassification.Trainers.SdcaMaximumEntr
opy("Label", "Features"))
.Append(MlContext.Transforms.Conversion.MapKeyToValue("PredictedLab
el"));
```

3. Lastly, we load in our test data, run the `MultiClassClassification`
   evaluation, and then output the four model evaluation properties, like this:

```
var testDataView =
MlContext.Data.LoadFromTextFile<Email>(testFileName, ',',
hasHeader: false);

var modelMetrics =
MlContext.MulticlassClassification.Evaluate(trainedModel.Transform(
testDataView));

Console.WriteLine($"MicroAccuracy:
{modelMetrics.MicroAccuracy:0.###}");
Console.WriteLine($"MacroAccuracy:
{modelMetrics.MacroAccuracy:0.###}");
Console.WriteLine($"LogLoss: {modelMetrics.LogLoss:#.###}");
Console.WriteLine($"LogLossReduction:
{modelMetrics.LogLossReduction:#.###}");
```

Running the application

To run the application, the process is nearly identical to the sample application in Chapter 3, *Regression Model*, with the addition of passing in the test dataset when training:

1. To run the training on the command line as we did in Chapter 1, *Getting Started with Machine Learning and ML.NET*, simply pass in the following command (assuming you are using the included sample dataset and test dataset):

```
PS chapter04-multiclass\bin\Debug\netcoreapp3.0> .\chapter04-
multiclass.exe train ..\..\..\Data\sampledata.csv
..\..\..\Data\testdata.csv
MicroAccuracy: 1
MacroAccuracy: 1
LogLoss: .1
LogLossReduction: .856
```

Note the expanded output to include several metric data points—we will go through what each one of these means at the end of this chapter.

2. After training the model, build a sample JSON file and save it as input.json, as follows:

```
{
    "Subject":"hello",
    "Body":"how is it?",
    "Sender":"joe@gmail.com"
}
```

3. To run the model with this file, simply pass in the filename to the built application, and the predicted output will show, as follows:

```
PS chapter04-multiclass\bin\Debug\netcoreapp3.0> .\chapter04-
multiclass.exe predict .\input.json
Based on input json:
{
"Subject":"hello",
"Body":"how is it?",
"Sender":"joe@gmail.com"
}
The email is predicted to be a "friend"
```

Feel free to modify the values and see how the prediction changes based on the dataset on which the model was trained. A few areas of experimentation from this point might be to:

- Add more sample and test data based on your own emails.
- Add more categories based on your own emails.
- Expand the features, such as the date of sending, and the IP address of the sender.

Evaluating a classification model

As discussed in previous chapters, evaluating a model is a critical part of the overall model-building process. A poorly trained model will only provide inaccurate predictions. Fortunately, ML.NET provides many popular attributes to calculate model accuracy, based on a test set at the time of training, to give you an idea of how well your model will perform in a production environment.

In ML.NET, as noted earlier in the sample applications, there are several properties that comprise the CalibratedBinaryClassificationMetrics class object. In Chapter 2, *Setting Up the ML.NET Environment*, we reviewed some of these properties. However, now that we have a more complex example and have learned how to evaluate regression models, let us dive into the following properties:

- Accuracy
- Area Under ROC Curve
- F1 Score
- Area Under Precision-Recall Curve

In addition, we will also look at the following four metrics returned by the MulticlassClassificationMetrics object used in the multi-class classification application:

- Micro Accuracy
- Macro Accuracy
- Log Loss
- Log-Loss Reduction

In the next sections, we will break down how these values are calculated, and detail the ideal values to look for.

Accuracy

Accuracy is the proportion of correct predictions to incorrect predictions in the test dataset.

You will want to be as close to a value of 100%, but not exactly 100%. As seen in our binary classification example, we received 88.89%—close to 100%, but not quite. If you see a 100% score when experimenting, you are more than likely seeing a case of overfitting.

Area Under ROC Curve

Area Under ROC Curve, also commonly referred to as AUC, is the measurement of the area under the curve.

As with Accuracy, a value close to 100% is ideal. If you are seeing values of less than 50%, your model either needs more features and/or more training data.

F1 Score

F1 Score is the harmonic mean of both precision and recall.

A value close to or equal to 100% is preferred. A value of 0 indicates your precision is completely inaccurate. As shown in our binary classification example, we received 87.50%.

Area Under Precision-Recall Curve

Area Under Precision-Recall Curve, also commonly referred to as AUPRC, is the measure of successful prediction. This value should be inspected when your dataset is imbalanced into one classification.

As with AUC and Accuracy, a value close to 100% is preferred, as this indicates you have a high recall. As shown in our binary classification example, we received a 100% AUPRC value.

Micro Accuracy

Micro Accuracy evaluates if every sample-class pair contributes equally to the accuracy metric.

A value close to or equal to 1 is preferred. As shown in our example application with the sample and test datasets, a value of 1 was achieved.

Macro Accuracy

Macro Accuracy evaluates if every class pair contributes equally to the accuracy metric.

A value close to or equal to 1 is preferred. As shown in our example application with the sample and test datasets, a value of 1 was achieved.

Log Loss

Log Loss is an evaluation metric describing the accuracy of the classifier. Log Loss takes into account the difference between the model's prediction and the actual classification.

A value close to 0 is preferred, as a value of 0 indicates the model's prediction on the test set is perfect. As shown in our example application with the sample and test datasets, a value of .1 was achieved.

Log-Loss Reduction

Log-Loss Reduction is simply an evaluation metric describing the accuracy of the classifier as compared to a random prediction.

A value close to or equal to 1 is preferred, as the model's relative accuracy improves as the value approaches 1. As shown in our example application with the sample and test datasets, a value of .856 was achieved, meaning the probability of guessing the correct answer is 85.6%.

Summary

Over the course of this chapter, we have deep-dived into classification models. We have also created and trained our first binary classification application, using FastTree and ML.NET, to predict how good a car's price is. We also created our first multi-class classification application using an SDCA trainer to categorize emails. Lastly, we also dove into how to evaluate a classification model and the various properties that ML.NET exposes to achieve a proper evaluation of your classification models.

In the next chapter, we will deep dive into clustering algorithms with ML.NET and creating a file-type classifier.

Clustering Model 5

With classification models behind us, it is now time to dive into clustering models. Currently, in ML.NET there is only one cluster algorithm, k-means. In this chapter, we will dive into k-means clustering as well as the various applications best suited to utilizing a clustering algorithm. In addition, we will build a new ML.NET clustering application that determines the type of a file simply by looking at the content. Finally, we will explore how to evaluate a k-means clustering model with the properties that ML.NET exposes.

In this chapter, we will cover the following topics:

- Breaking down the k-means algorithm
- Creating the clustering application
- Evaluating a k-means model

Breaking down the k-means algorithm

As mentioned in Chapter 1, *Getting Started with Machine Learning and ML.NET*, k-means clustering, by definition, is an unsupervised learning algorithm. This means that data is grouped into clusters based on the data provided to the model for training. In this section, we will dive into a number of use cases for clustering and the k-means trainer.

Use cases for clustering

Clustering, as you may be beginning to realize, has numerous applications where the output categorizes similar outputs into groups of similar data points.

Some of its potential applications include the following:

- Natural disaster tracking such as earthquakes or hurricanes and creating clusters of high-danger zones
- Book or document grouping based on the authors, subject matter, and sources
- Grouping customer data into targeted marketing predictions
- Search result grouping of similar results that other users found useful

In addition, it has numerous other applications such as predicting malware families or medical purposes for cancer research.

Diving into the k-means trainer

The k-means trainer used in ML.NET is based on the Yinyang method as opposed to a classic k-means implementation. Like some of the trainers we have looked at in previous chapters, all of the input must be of the Float type. In addition, all input must be normalized into a single feature vector. Fortunately, the k-means trainer is included in the main ML.NET NuGet package; therefore, no additional dependencies are required.

> To learn more about the Yinyang implementation, Microsoft Research published a white paper here: https://www.microsoft.com/en-us/research/wp-content/uploads/2016/02/ding15.pdf.

Take a look at the following diagram, showing three clusters and a data point:

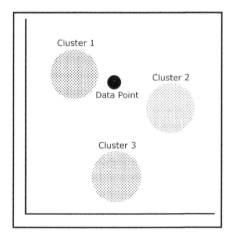

In clustering, each of these clusters represents a grouping of similar data points. With k-means clustering (and other clustering algorithms), the distances between the data point and each of the clusters are the measures of which cluster the model will return. For k-means clustering specifically, it uses the center point of each of these clusters (also called a centroid) and then calculates the distance to the data point. The smallest of these values is the predicted cluster.

For the k-means trainer, it can be initialized in one of three ways. One way is to utilize a randomized initialization—as you have probably guessed, this can lead to randomized prediction results. Another way is to utilize k-means++, which strives to produce O(log K) predictions. Lastly, k-means||, the default method in ML.NET, uses a parallel method to reduce the number of passes required to initialize.

For more information on k-means||, you can refer to a paper published by Stanford, which explains it in detail: https://theory.stanford.edu/~sergei/papers/vldb12-kmpar.pdf.

For more information on k-means++, you can refer to a paper published by Stanford in 2006, explaining it in detail: http://ilpubs.stanford.edu:8090/778/1/2006-13.pdf.

We will demonstrate this trainer in the example application in the next section.

Creating the clustering application

As mentioned earlier, the application we will be creating is a file type classifier. Given a set of attributes statically extracted from a file, the prediction will return if it is a document, an executable, or a script. For those of you who have used the Linux `file` command, this is a simplified version but based on machine learning. The attributes included in this example aren't the definitive list of attributes, nor should they be used as-is in a production environment; however, you could use this as a starting point for creating a true ML-based replacement for the Linux `file` command.

As with previous chapters, the completed project code, sample dataset, and project files can be downloaded here: https://github.com/PacktPublishing/Hands-On-Machine-Learning-With-ML.NET/tree/master/chapter05.

Exploring the project architecture

Building on the project architecture and code we created in previous chapters, the major change architecturally is in the feature extraction being done on both the training and test sets.

Here, you will find the Visual Studio Solution Explorer view of the project. The new additions to the solution are the `FileTypes`, `FileData`, and `FilePrediction` files that we will review later on in this section:

The `sampledata.csv` file contains 80 rows of random files I had on my system, comprising 30 Windows executables, 20 PowerShell scripts, and 20 Word documents. Feel free to adjust the data to fit your own observations or to adjust the trained model. Here is a snippet of the data:

```
0,1,1,0
0,1,1,0
0,1,1,0
```

```
2,0,0,0
2,0,0,0
2,0,0,0
2,0,0,0
2,0,0,0
2,0,0,0
2,0,0,0
2,0,0,0
2,0,0,0
2,0,0,0
2,0,0,0
1,1,0,1
1,1,0,1
1,1,0,1
1,1,0,1
```

Each of these rows contains the value for the properties in the newly created `FileData` class that we will review later on in this chapter.

In addition to this, we added the `testdata.csv` file, which contains additional data points to test the newly trained model against and evaluate. The breakdown was even with 10 Windows executables, 10 PowerShell scripts, and 10 Word documents. Here is a snippet of the data inside `testdata.csv`:

```
0,1,1,0
0,1,1,0
2,0,0,0
2,0,0,0
2,0,0,0
2,0,0,0
2,0,0,0
2,0,0,0
1,1,0,1
```

Diving into the code

For this application, as noted in the previous section, we are building on top of the work completed in Chapter 4, *Classification Model*. For this deep dive, we are going to focus solely on the code that was changed for this application.

Classes that were changed or added are as follows:

- `Constants`
- `BaseML`
- `FileTypes`
- `FileData`
- `FileTypePrediction`
- `FeatureExtractor`
- `Predictor`
- `Trainer`
- `Program`

The Constants class

The `Constants` class has been changed to save the model to `chapter5.mdl`, in addition to supporting a feature-extracted `testdata.csv` variable. The following code block reflects these changes:

```
namespace chapter05.Common
{
    public class Constants
    {
        public const string MODEL_FILENAME = "chapter5.mdl";

        public const string SAMPLE_DATA = "sampledata.csv";

        public const string TEST_DATA = "testdata.csv";
    }
}
```

The BaseML class

The sole change in the `BaseML` class is the addition of the `FEATURES` variable. By using a variable here, we can remove the use of a magic string in our `Trainer` class (we will discuss this later in this section):

```
protected const string FEATURES = "Features";
```

The FileTypes enumeration

The `FileTypes` enumeration contains a strongly typed method for mapping our classifications and a numeric value. As we discovered in our previous examples, utilizing an enumeration as opposed to magic or constant values provides better flexibility, as shown here and throughout the remaining classes:

```
namespace chapter05.Enums
{
    public enum FileTypes
    {
        Executable = 0,
        Document = 1,
        Script = 2
    }
}
```

The FileData class

The `FileData` class is the container class that contains the data to both predict and train our model:

1. First, we add constant values for `True` and `False` since k-means requires floating-point values:

```
public class FileData
{
    private const float TRUE = 1.0f;
    private const float FALSE = 0.0f;
```

2. Next, we create a constructor that supports both our prediction and training. We optionally pass in the filename for the training to provide a label, in this case, ps1, exe, and doc for scripts, executables, and documents, respectively. We also call helper methods to determine whether the file is binary, or whether it starts with MZ or PK:

```
public FileData(Span<byte> data, string fileName = null)
{
    // Used for training purposes only
    if (!string.IsNullOrEmpty(fileName))
    {
        if (fileName.Contains("ps1"))
        {
            Label = (float) FileTypes.Script;
```

```
        } else if (fileName.Contains("exe"))
        {
            Label = (float) FileTypes.Executable;
        } else if (fileName.Contains("doc"))
        {
            Label = (float) FileTypes.Document;
        }
    }

    IsBinary = HasBinaryContent(data) ? TRUE : FALSE;

    IsMZHeader = HasHeaderBytes(data.Slice(0, 2), "MZ") ? TRUE :
                            FALSE;

    IsPKHeader = HasHeaderBytes(data.Slice(0, 2), "PK") ? TRUE :
                            FALSE;
}
```

MZ and PK are considered to be magic numbers of Windows executables and modern Microsoft Office files. Magic numbers are unique byte strings that are found at the beginning of every file. In this case, both are simply two bytes. When performing analysis on files, making quick determinations is crucial for performance. For the keen reader, PK is also the magic number for ZIP. Modern Microsoft Office documents are actually ZIP archives. For the sake of simplicity in this example, PK is used as opposed to performing an additional level of detection.

3. Next, we also add an additional constructor to support the hard truth setting of values. We will deep dive into the purpose of this addition later on in this section:

```
/// <summary>
/// Used for mapping cluster ids to results only
/// </summary>
/// <param name="fileType"></param>
public FileData(FileTypes fileType)
{
    Label = (float)fileType;

    switch (fileType)
    {
        case FileTypes.Document:
            IsBinary = TRUE;
            IsMZHeader = FALSE;
            IsPKHeader = TRUE;
            break;
        case FileTypes.Executable:
```

```
                IsBinary = TRUE;
                IsMZHeader = TRUE;
                IsPKHeader = FALSE;
                break;
            case FileTypes.Script:
                IsBinary = FALSE;
                IsMZHeader = FALSE;
                IsPKHeader = FALSE;
                break;
        }
    }
```

4. Next, we implement our two helper methods. The first, `HasBinaryContent`, as the name implies, takes the raw binary data and searches for non-text characters to ensure it is a binary file. Secondly, we define `HasHeaderBytes`; this method takes an array of bytes, converts it into a UTF8 string, and then checks to see whether the string matches the string passed in:

```
private static bool HasBinaryContent(Span<byte> fileContent) =>
System.Text.Encoding.UTF8.GetString(fileContent.ToArray()).Any(a =>
char.IsControl(a) && a != '\r' && a != '\n');

private static bool HasHeaderBytes(Span<byte> data, string match)
=> System.Text.Encoding.UTF8.GetString(data) == match;
```

5. Next, we add the properties used for prediction, training, and testing:

```
[ColumnName("Label")]
public float Label { get; set; }

public float IsBinary { get; set; }

public float IsMZHeader { get; set; }

public float IsPKHeader { get; set; }
```

6. Lastly, we override the `ToString` method to be used with the feature extraction:

```
public override string ToString() =>
$"{Label},{IsBinary},{IsMZHeader},{IsPKHeader}";
```

The FileTypePrediction class

The `FileTypePrediction` class contains the properties mapped to our prediction output. In k-means clustering, the `PredictedClusterId` property stores the closest cluster found. In addition to this, the `Distances` array contains the distances from the data point to each of the clusters:

```
using Microsoft.ML.Data;

namespace chapter05.ML.Objects
{
    public class FileTypePrediction
    {
        [ColumnName("PredictedLabel")]
        public uint PredictedClusterId;

        [ColumnName("Score")]
        public float[] Distances;
    }
}
```

The FeatureExtractor class

The `FeatureExtractor` class that we utilized in the logistic regression example from Chapter 3, *Regression Model*, has been adapted to support both test and training data extraction:

1. First, we generalize the extraction to take the folder path and the output file. As noted earlier, we also pass in the filename, providing the `Labeling` to occur cleanly inside the `FileData` class:

```
private void ExtractFolder(string folderPath, string outputFile)
{
    if (!Directory.Exists(folderPath))
    {
        Console.WriteLine($"{folderPath} does not exist");

        return;
    }

    var files = Directory.GetFiles(folderPath);

    using (var streamWriter =
        new StreamWriter(Path.Combine(AppContext.BaseDirectory,
                            $"../../../Data/{outputFile}")))
```

```
    {
        foreach (var file in files)
        {
            var extractedData = new FileData(
                            File.ReadAllBytes(file), file);

            streamWriter.WriteLine(extractedData.ToString());
        }
    }

    Console.WriteLine($"Extracted {files.Length} to {outputFile}");
    }
```

2. Lastly, we take the two parameters from the command line (called from the Program class) and simply call the preceding method a second time:

```
public void Extract(string trainingPath, string testPath)
{
    ExtractFolder(trainingPath, Constants.SAMPLE_DATA);
    ExtractFolder(testPath, Constants.TEST_DATA);
}
```

The Predictor class

There are a couple of changes in this class to handle the file type prediction scenario:

1. First, we add a helper method, GetClusterToMap, which maps known values to the prediction clusters. Note the use of Enum.GetValues here; as you add more file types, this method does not need to be modified:

```
private Dictionary<uint, FileTypes>
GetClusterToMap(PredictionEngineBase<FileData, FileTypePrediction>
predictionEngine)
{
    var map = new Dictionary<uint, FileTypes>();

    var fileTypes = Enum.GetValues(
                        typeof(FileTypes)).Cast<FileTypes>();

    foreach (var fileType in fileTypes)
    {
        var fileData = new FileData(fileType);

        var prediction = predictionEngine.Predict(fileData);

        map.Add(prediction.PredictedClusterId, fileType);
```

```
        }

        return map;
    }
```

2. Next, we pass in the `FileData` and `FileTypePrediction` types into the `CreatePredictionEngine` method to create our prediction engine. Then, we read the file in as a binary file and pass these bytes into the constructor of `FileData` prior to running the prediction and mapping initialization:

```
var predictionEngine =
MlContext.Model.CreatePredictionEngine<FileData,
FileTypePrediction>(mlModel);

var fileData = new FileData(File.ReadAllBytes(inputDataFile));

var prediction = predictionEngine.Predict(fileData);

var mapping = GetClusterToMap(predictionEngine);
```

3. Lastly, we need to adjust the output to match the output that a k-means prediction returns, including the Euclidean distances:

```
Console.WriteLine(
    $"Based on input file: {inputDataFile}{Environment.NewLine}
                        {Environment.NewLine}" +
    $"Feature Extraction: {fileData}{Environment.NewLine}
                        {Environment.NewLine}" +
    $"The file is predicted to be a {
                        mapping[prediction.PredictedClusterId]}
                        {Environment.NewLine}");

Console.WriteLine("Distances from all clusters:");

for (uint x = 0; x < prediction.Distances.Length; x++) {
    Console.WriteLine($"{mapping[x+1]}:
                        {prediction.Distances[x]}");
}
```

The Trainer class

Inside the `Trainer` class, several modifications need to be made to support k-means classification:

1. The first change is the addition of a `GetDataView` helper method, which builds the `IDataView` object from the columns previously defined in the `FileData` class:

```
private IDataView GetDataView(string fileName)
{
    return MlContext.Data.LoadFromTextFile(path: fileName,
        columns: new[]
        {
            new TextLoader.Column(nameof(FileData.Label),
                                    DataKind.Single, 0),
            new TextLoader.Column(nameof(FileData.IsBinary),
                                    DataKind.Single, 1),
            new TextLoader.Column(nameof(FileData.IsMZHeader),
                                    DataKind.Single, 2),
            new TextLoader.Column(nameof(FileData.IsPKHeader),
                                    DataKind.Single, 3)
        },
        hasHeader: false,
        separatorChar: ',');
}
```

2. We then build the data process pipeline, transforming the columns into a single `Features` column:

```
var trainingDataView = GetDataView(trainingFileName);

var dataProcessPipeline = MlContext.Transforms.Concatenate(
    FEATURES,
    nameof(FileData.IsBinary),
    nameof(FileData.IsMZHeader),
    nameof(FileData.IsPKHeader));
```

3. We can then create the k-means trainer with a cluster size of 3 and create the model:

```
var trainer = MlContext.Clustering.Trainers.KMeans(
            featureColumnName: FEATURES, numberOfClusters: 3);
var trainingPipeline = dataProcessPipeline.Append(trainer);
var trainedModel = trainingPipeline.Fit(trainingDataView);
```

```
MlContext.Model.Save(trainedModel, trainingDataView.Schema,
ModelPath);
```

 The default value for the number of clusters is 5. An interesting experiment to run based either on this dataset or one modified by you is to see how the prediction results change by adjusting this value.

4. Now we evaluate the model we just trained using the testing dataset:

```
var testingDataView = GetDataView(testingFileName);

IDataView testDataView = trainedModel.Transform(testingDataView);

ClusteringMetrics modelMetrics = MlContext.Clustering.Evaluate(
    data: testDataView,
    labelColumnName: "Label",
    scoreColumnName: "Score",
    featureColumnName: FEATURES);
```

5. Finally, we output all of the classification metrics, each of which we will detail in the next section:

```
Console.WriteLine($"Average Distance:
{modelMetrics.AverageDistance}");
Console.WriteLine($"Davies Bould Index:
{modelMetrics.DaviesBouldinIndex}");
Console.WriteLine($"Normalized Mutual Information:
{modelMetrics.NormalizedMutualInformation}");
```

The Program class

The Program class, as mentioned in previous chapters, is the main entry point for our application. The only change in the Program class is the help text to indicate usage for the extract to accept the test folder path for extraction:

```
if (args.Length < 2)
{
    Console.WriteLine($"Invalid arguments passed in,
                    exiting.{Environment.NewLine}{Environment.NewLine}
                    Usage:{Environment.NewLine}" +
                $"predict <path to input file>{Environment.NewLine}"+
                $"or {Environment.NewLine}" +
                $"train <path to training data file>
                    <path to test data file>{Environment.NewLine}" +
```

```
                          $"or {Environment.NewLine}" +
                          $"extract <path to training folder>
                             <path to test folder>{Environment.NewLine}");

        return;
    }
```

Finally, we modify the switch/case statement to support the additional parameter to the extract method to support both the training and test datasets:

```
switch (args[0])
{
    case "extract":
        new FeatureExtractor().Extract(args[1], args[2]);
        break;
    case "predict":
        new Predictor().Predict(args[1]);
        break;
    case "train":
        new Trainer().Train(args[1], args[2]);
        break;
    default:
        Console.WriteLine($"{args[0]} is an invalid option");
        break;
}
```

Running the application

To run the application, the process is nearly identical to Chapter 3, *Regression Model*'s example application with the addition of passing in the test dataset when training:

1. To run the training on the command line as we did in previous chapters, simply pass in the following command (assuming you have added two sets of files; one each for your training and test sets):

   ```
   PS chapter05\bin\Debug\netcoreapp3.0> .\chapter05.exe extract
   ..\..\..\TrainingData\ ..\..\..\TestData\
   Extracted 80 to sampledata.csv
   Extracted 30 to testdata.csv
   ```

Included in the code repository are two pre-feature extracted files (`sampledata.csv` and `testdata.csv`) to allow you to train a model without performing your own feature extraction. If you would like to perform your own feature extraction, create a `TestData` and `TrainingData` folder. Populate these folders with a sampling of **PowerShell (PS1)**, **Windows Executables (EXE)** and **Microsoft Word documents (DOCX)**.

2. After extracting the data, we must then train the model by passing in the newly created `sampledata.csv` and `testdata.csv` files:

```
PS chapter05\bin\Debug\netcoreapp3.0> .\chapter05.exe train
..\..\..\Data\sampledata.csv ..\..\..\Data\testdata.csv
Average Distance: 0
Davies Bould Index: 0
Normalized Mutual Information: 1
```

3. To run the model with this file, simply pass in the filename to the built application (in this case, the compiled `chapter05.exe` is used) and the predicted output will show:

```
PS chapter05\bin\Debug\netcoreapp3.0> .\chapter05.exe predict
.\chapter05.exe
Based on input file: .\chapter05.exe

Feature Extraction: 0,1,1,0

The file is predicted to be a Executable

Distances from all clusters:
Executable: 0
Script: 2
Document: 2
```

Note the expanded output to include several metric data points—we will go through what each one of these means at the end of this chapter.

Feel free to modify the values and see how the prediction changes based on the dataset that the model was trained on. A few areas of experimentation from this point could include the following:

- Adding some additional features to increase the prediction accuracy
- Adding additional file types to the clusters such as video or audio
- Adding a new range of files to generate new sample and test data

Evaluating a k-means model

As discussed in previous chapters, evaluating a model is a critical part of the overall model-building process. A poorly trained model will only provide inaccurate predictions. Fortunately, ML.NET provides many popular attributes to calculate model accuracy based on a test set at the time of training to give you an idea of how well your model will perform in a production environment.

In ML.NET, as noted in the example application, there are three properties that comprise the ClusteringMetrics class object. Let's dive into the properties exposed in the ClusteringMetrics object:

- Average distance
- The Davies-Bouldin index
- Normalized mutual information

In the next sections, we will break down how these values are calculated and the ideal values to look for.

Average distance

Also referred to as the **average score** is the distance from the center of a cluster to the test data. The value, of type double, will decrease as the number of clusters increases, effectively creating clusters for the edge cases. In addition to this, a value of 0, such as the one found in our example, is possible when your features create distinct clusters. This means that, if you find yourself seeing poor prediction performance, you should increase the number of clusters.

The Davies-Bouldin Index

The Davies-Bouldin Index is another measure for the quality of the clustering. Specifically, the Davies-Bouldin Index measures the scatter of cluster separation with values ranging from 0 to 1 (of type double), with a value of 0 being ideal (as was the case of our example).

 For more details on the Davies-Bouldin Index, specifically the math behind the algorithm, a good resource can be found here: `https://en.wikipedia.org/wiki/Davies%E2%80%93Bouldin_index`.

Normalized mutual information

The normalized mutual information metric is used to measure the mutual dependence of the feature variables.

The range of values is from 0 to 1 (the type is of double)—closer to or equal to 1 is ideal, akin to the model we trained earlier in this chapter.

 For more details on normalized mutual information along with the math behind the algorithm, please read `http://en.wikipedia.org/wiki/Mutual_information#Normalized_variants`.

Summary

Over the course of this chapter, we dove into ML.NET's clustering support via the k-means clustering algorithm. We have also created and trained our first clustering application using k-means to predict what file type a file is. Lastly, we dove into how to evaluate a k-means clustering model and the various properties that ML.NET exposes to achieve a proper evaluation of a k-means clustering model.

In the next chapter, we will deep dive into anomaly detection algorithms with ML.NET by creating a login anomaly predictor.

Anomaly Detection Model 6

With k-means clustering models behind us, it is now time to dive into anomaly detection models. Anomaly detection is one of the newer additions to ML.NET, and specifically, time-series transforms. In this chapter, we will dive into anomaly detection and the various applications best suited to utilizing anomaly detection. In addition, we will build two new example applications: one anomaly detection application that determines whether the login attempt is abnormally demonstrating the randomized PCA trainer, and one that demonstrates time series in a network traffic anomaly detection application. Finally, we will explore how to evaluate an anomaly detection model with the properties that ML.NET exposes.

In this chapter, we will cover the following topics:

- Breaking down anomaly detection
- Creating a time series application
- Creating an anomaly detection application
- Evaluating an anomaly detection model

Breaking down anomaly detection

As mentioned in Chapter 1, *Getting Started with Machine Learning and ML.NET*, anomaly detection, by definition, is an unsupervised learning algorithm. This means that the algorithm will train on data and look for data that does not fit the normal data. In this section, we will dive into use cases for anomaly detection and into the various trainers available for anomaly detection in ML.NET.

Use cases for anomaly detection

Anomaly detection, as you might have realized already, has numerous applications where data is available but it is unknown whether there is an anomaly in the data. Without needing to do manual spot-checking, anomaly detection algorithms train on this data and determine whether there are any anomalies. ML.NET provides various anomaly detection values to look at programmatically inside of your application. We will review these values later on in this chapter to better ensure that any detection is not a false positive.

Some of the potential applications best suited for anomaly detection include the following:

- Sales forecasting
- Stock market
- Fraud detection
- Anticipating the failure of a device due to various factors
- Cyber-security applications for remote connections and network traffic login history, such as the example application that we will dive into later

Diving into the randomized PCA trainer

The randomized PCA trainer is the only traditional trainer for anomaly detection found in ML.NET at the time of writing. The randomized PCA trainer requires normalization of the values; however, caching is not necessary and no additional NuGet packages are required to utilize the trainer.

Similar to other algorithms, the input is a known vector size of the Float type. The output comprises two properties: Score and PredictedLabel. The Score value is of the Float type, non-negative, and unbounded. In contrast, the PredictedLabel property indicates a valid anomaly based on the threshold set; a value of true indicates an anomaly, while a value of false indicates otherwise. ML.NET's default threshold is 0.5, which can be adjusted via the ChangeModelThreshold method. Effectively, values higher than the threshold return true, and false if they are lower.

Under the hood, the algorithm uses eigenvectors to estimate the subspace containing the normal class and then computes the normalized difference between the actual feature vector and the projected feature vector in that subspace. Put simply, the algorithm finds edge cases if the computed error is not close to 0. If it finds the error is close to 0, it is considered a normal data point (that is, a non-anomaly).

We will demonstrate this trainer in the second example application later on in this chapter, by detecting login anomalies.

 If you would like to deep dive further into randomized PCA, the following paper is a great resource: `https://web.stanford.edu/group/mmds/slides2010/Martinsson.pdf`.

Diving into time series transforms

Unlike other algorithms found in this book and ML.NET itself, time series support was added as a series of transforms to be applied to your training and test data. Time series, as mentioned previously, is also one of the newer additions to ML.NET, being added in 1.2.0.

In ML.NET, times series transforms are grouped into the `TimeSeriesCatalog` class. There are six different methods inside this class:

- `DetectAnomalyBySrCnn`: Detects anomalies with the SRCNN algorithm
- `DetectChangePointBySsa`: Detects anomalies with the **Singular Spectrum Analysis (SSA)** algorithm on change points
- `DetectIidChangePoint`: Detects changes to predict change points with an **independent identically distributed (i.i.d)** algorithm
- `DetectIidSpike`: Detects changes with an i.i.d algorithm but predicts spikes instead of change points
- `DetectSpikeBySsa`: Detects spikes using the SSA algorithm
- `ForecastBySsa`: Uses the SSA algorithm for a singular variable- (commonly referred to as univariate-) based time series forecasting

Depending on the application, you may want to look for spikes of data changes or points of change (on the upward or downward spiral). In this chapter's example on time series, we will be looking for spikes in network transfer over time utilizing `DetectSpikeBySsa`.

For more information on forecasting with SSA, a great resource can be found here: `http://arxiv.org/pdf/1206.6910.pdf`.

Creating a time series application

As mentioned earlier, the application we will be creating is a network traffic anomaly detector. Given a set of attributes relating to the network traffic amount (in bytes), the application will use that data to find anomalies in the amount of traffic for a given checkpoint. As with other applications, this is not meant to power the next ML network traffic anomaly detection product; however, it will show you how to use time series in ML.NET, specifically to detect spikes with SSA.

As with previous chapters, the completed project code, sample dataset, and project files can be downloaded here: `https://github.com/PacktPublishing/Hands-On-Machine-Learning-With-ML.NET/tree/master/chapter06-time-series`.

Exploring the project architecture

Building on the project architecture and code we created in previous chapters, the bulk of the changes are in the training of the model as time series requires a fairly significant paradigm shift from what we have reviewed in previous chapters. In addition to this, when using time series transforms, you will need to add the `Microsoft.ML.TimeSeries` NuGet package if you are creating a project from scratch. The example application available in the GitHub repository has this package already included.

In the following screenshot, you will find the Visual Studio Solution Explorer view of the project. The new additions to the solution are the `NetworkTrafficHistory` and `NetworkTrafficPrediction` files, which we will review later on in this section:

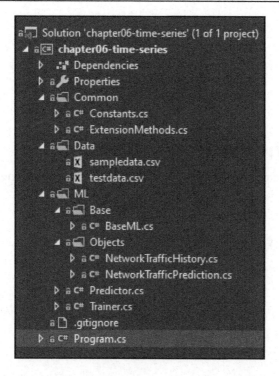

The `sampledata.csv` file contains eight rows of network traffic data. Feel free to adjust the data to fit your own observations or to adjust the trained model. Here is a snippet of the data:

```
laptop,2019-11-14T11:13:23,1500
laptop,2019-11-15T11:13:23,1000
laptop,2019-11-16T11:13:23,1100
laptop,2019-11-17T11:13:23,1600
laptop,2019-11-18T11:13:23,1000
laptop,2019-11-19T11:13:23,1100
laptop,2019-11-20T11:13:23,1000
laptop,2019-11-21T11:13:23,1000
```

Each of these rows contains the values for the properties in the newly created `NetworkTrafficHistory` class, which we will review later on in this chapter.

In addition to this, we have added the `testdata.csv` file, which contains additional data points to test the newly trained model against and evaluate. Here is a snippet of the data inside of `testdata.csv`:

```
laptop,2019-11-22T11:13:23,1000
laptop,2019-11-23T11:13:23,1100
```

```
laptop,2019-11-24T11:13:23,1200
laptop,2019-11-25T11:13:23,1300
laptop,2019-11-26T11:13:23,1400
laptop,2019-11-27T11:13:23,3000
laptop,2019-11-28T11:13:23,1500
laptop,2019-11-29T11:13:23,1600
```

Diving into the code

For this application, as noted in the previous section, we are building on top of the work completed in Chapter 5, *Clustering Model*. For this deep dive, we are going to focus solely on the code that was changed for this application.

Classes that were changed or added are as follows:

- NetworkTrafficHistory
- NetworkTrafficPrediction
- Predictor
- Trainer
- Program

The NetworkTrafficHistory class

The NetworkTrafficHistory class is the container class that contains the data to both predict and train our model. As described in previous chapters, the number in the LoadColumn decorator maps to the index in the CSV files. As noted earlier, anomaly detection in ML.NET requires the use of a single floating-point value; in this case, it is the BytesTransferred property:

```
using System;

using Microsoft.ML.Data;

namespace chapter06.ML.Objects
{
    public class NetworkTrafficHistory
    {
        [LoadColumn(0)]
        public string HostMachine { get; set; }

        [LoadColumn(1)]
        public DateTime Timestamp { get; set; }
```

```
        [LoadColumn(2)]
        public float BytesTransferred { get; set; }
    }
}
```

The NetworkTrafficPrediction class

The `NetworkTrafficPrediction` class contains the properties mapped to our prediction output. The `VectorType(3)` function holds the alert, score, and p-value. We will review these values later on in this section:

```
using Microsoft.ML.Data;

namespace chapter06.ML.Objects
{
    public class NetworkTrafficPrediction
    {
        [VectorType(3)]
        public double[] Prediction { get; set; }
    }
}
```

The Predictor class

There are a couple of changes to make to this class in order to handle the network traffic prediction scenario:

1. First, we create our prediction engine with the `NetworkTrafficHistory` and `NetworkHistoryPrediction` types:

```
var predictionEngine =
MlContext.Model.CreatePredictionEngine<NetworkTrafficHistory,
NetworkTrafficPrediction>(mlModel);
```

2. Next, we read the input file into an `IDataView` variable (note the override to use a comma as `separatorChar`):

```
var inputData =
MlContext.Data.LoadFromTextFile<NetworkTrafficHistory>(inputDataFil
e, separatorChar: ',');
```

3. Next, we take the newly created `IDataView` variable and get an enumerable based off of that data view:

```
var rows =
MlContext.Data.CreateEnumerable<NetworkTrafficHistory>(inputData,
false);
```

4. Lastly, we need to run the prediction and then output the results of the model run:

```
Console.WriteLine($"Based on input file ({inputDataFile}):");

foreach (var row in rows)
{
    var prediction = predictionEngine.Predict(row);

    Console.Write($"HOST: {row.HostMachine}
                TIMESTAMP: {row.Timestamp}
                TRANSFER: {row.BytesTransferred} ");
    Console.Write($"ALERT: {prediction.Prediction[0]}
                SCORE: {prediction.Prediction[1]:f2}
                P-VALUE: {prediction.Prediction[2]:F2}
                    {Environment.NewLine}");
}
```

With `Transform` only returning the three-element vector, the original row data is output to give context.

The Trainer class

Inside the `Trainer` class, several modifications need to be made to support the time series transform. In many ways, a simplification is required. The removal of the evaluation and testing data load is performed:

1. The first addition is of the four variables to send to the transform:

```
private const int PvalueHistoryLength = 3;
private const int SeasonalityWindowSize = 3;
private const int TrainingWindowSize = 7;
private const int Confidence = 98;
```

The training window size must be greater than twice the p-value history length due to a constraint in the ML.NET library at the time of writing.

2. We then build the `DataView` object from the CSV training file:

```
var trainingDataView = GetDataView(trainingFileName);
```

3. We can then create SSA spike detection:

```
var trainingPipeLine = MlContext.Transforms.DetectSpikeBySsa(
    nameof(NetworkTrafficPrediction.Prediction),
    nameof(NetworkTrafficHistory.BytesTransferred),
    confidence: Confidence,
    pvalueHistoryLength: PvalueHistoryLength,
    trainingWindowSize: TrainingWindowSize,
    seasonalityWindowSize: SeasonalityWindowSize);
```

4. Now, we fit the model on the training data and save the model:

```
ITransformer trainedModel = trainingPipeLine.Fit(trainingDataView);

MlContext.Model.Save(trainedModel, trainingDataView.Schema,
ModelPath);

Console.WriteLine("Model trained");
```

The Program class

Given that the training only requires the training data, some modifications to the `Program` class have to be performed:

1. The help text needs to be updated to reflect the new usage:

```
if (args.Length < 2)
{
    Console.WriteLine(
        $"Invalid arguments passed in, exiting.{Environment.NewLine}
                {Environment.NewLine}Usage:{Environment.NewLine}" +
        $"predict <path to input file>{Environment.NewLine}" +
        $"or {Environment.NewLine}" +
        $"train <path to training data file>{Environment.NewLine}");

    return;
}
```

2. In addition, the switch case statement needs to be updated to reflect the single argument passed for the prediction:

```
switch (args[0])
{
    case "predict":
        new Predictor().Predict(args[1]);
        break;
    case "train":
        new Trainer().Train(args[1]);
        break;
    default:
        Console.WriteLine($"{args[0]} is an invalid option");
        break;
}
```

Running the application

To run the application, the process we use is nearly identical to Chapter 3, *Regression Model*'s example application:

1. After preparing the data, we must train the model by passing in the newly created sampledata.csv file:

   ```
   PS chapter06-time-series\bin\Debug\netcoreapp3.0> .\chapter06-time-
   series.exe train ..\..\..\Data\sampledata.csv
   Model trained
   ```

2. To run the model with this file, simply pass in the testdata.csv file mentioned earlier into the newly built application, and the predicted output will show the following:

   ```
   PS bin\debug\netcoreapp3.0> .\chapter06-time-series.exe predict
   ..\..\..\Data\testdata.csv
   Based on input file (..\..\..\Data\testdata.csv):
   HOST: laptop TIMESTAMP: 11/22/2019 11:13:23 AM TRANSFER: 1000
   ALERT: 0 SCORE: 46.07 P-VALUE: 0.50
   HOST: laptop TIMESTAMP: 11/23/2019 11:13:23 AM TRANSFER: 1100
   ALERT: 0 SCORE: 131.36 P-VALUE: 0.00
   HOST: laptop TIMESTAMP: 11/24/2019 11:13:23 AM TRANSFER: 1200
   ALERT: 0 SCORE: 180.44 P-VALUE: 0.06
   HOST: laptop TIMESTAMP: 11/25/2019 11:13:23 AM TRANSFER: 1300
   ALERT: 0 SCORE: 195.42 P-VALUE: 0.17
   HOST: laptop TIMESTAMP: 11/26/2019 11:13:23 AM TRANSFER: 1400
   ALERT: 0 SCORE: 201.15 P-VALUE: 0.22
   ```

```
HOST: laptop TIMESTAMP: 11/27/2019 11:13:23 AM TRANSFER: 3000
ALERT: 1 SCORE: 1365.42 P-VALUE: 0.00
HOST: laptop TIMESTAMP: 11/28/2019 11:13:23 AM TRANSFER: 1500
ALERT: 0 SCORE: -324.58 P-VALUE: 0.11
HOST: laptop TIMESTAMP: 11/29/2019 11:13:23 AM TRANSFER: 1600
ALERT: 0 SCORE: -312.93 P-VALUE: 0.25
```

The output includes the three data points: HOST, TIMESTAMP, and TRANSFER. The new additions are ALERT, SCORE, and P-VALUE. ALERT values of nonzero indicate an anomaly. SCORE is a numeric representation of the anomaly score; a higher value indicates a spike. P-VALUE, a value between 0 and 1, is the distance between the current point and the average point. A value closer or equal to 0 is another indication of a spike. When evaluating your model and efficacy, using these three data points together you can be guaranteed a true spike, effectively reducing the potential false positive count.

Feel free to modify the values and explore how the prediction changes based on the dataset that the model was trained on. A few areas of experimentation from this point might be as follows:

- Adding more specific data points such as an IP address
- Adding diversification and more data points to the training and test data

Creating an anomaly detection application

As mentioned earlier, the application we will be creating is a login anomaly detector. Given a set of attributes relating to the login, the application will use that data to find anomalies such as unusual login times. As with other applications, this is not meant to power the next ML login anomaly detection product; however, it will show you how to use anomaly detection in ML.NET.

As with previous chapters, the completed project code, sample dataset, and project files can be downloaded here: https://github.com/PacktPublishing/Hands-On-Machine-Learning-With-ML.NET/tree/master/chapter06.

Exploring the project architecture

Building on the project architecture and code we created in previous chapters, the bulk of the changes in this example are in the training of the model.

In the following screenshot, you will find the Visual Studio Solution Explorer view of the project. The new additions to the solution are the LoginHistory and LoginPrediction files, which we will review later on in this section:

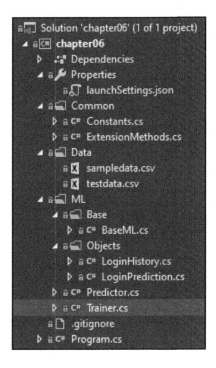

The sampledata.csv file contains 10 rows of login data. Feel free to adjust the data to fit your own observations or to adjust the trained model. Here is a snippet of the data:

```
0,1,0,1,1,0
0,1,0,1,1,0
0,0,1,0,1,0
0,0,1,0,1,0
0,0,1,1,0,1
1,1,0,1,1,0
1,1,0,1,1,0
1,0,1,0,1,0
1,0,1,0,1,1
1,0,1,1,0,0
```

Each of these rows contains the values for the properties in the newly created `LoginHistory` class, which we will review later on in this chapter.

In addition to this, we added the `testdata.csv` file, which contains additional data points to test the newly trained model against and evaluate. Here is a snippet of the data inside of `testdata.csv`:

```
0,1,0,1,1,0
0,1,0,1,1,0
0,0,1,0,1,0
0,0,1,0,1,0
0,0,1,1,0,1
1,1,0,1,1,0
1,1,0,1,1,0
1,0,1,0,1,0
1,0,1,0,1,1
1,0,1,1,0,0
```

Diving into the code

For this application, as noted in the previous section, we are building on top of the work completed in Chapter 5, *Clustering Model*. For this deep dive, we are going to focus solely on the code that was changed for this application.

Classes that were changed or added are as follows:

- Constants
- LoginHistory
- LoginPrediction
- Predictor
- Trainer

The Constants class

The `Constants` class has been changed to save the model to `chapter6.mdl`. The following code block reflects these changes:

```
namespace chapter06.Common
{
    public class Constants
    {
        public const string MODEL_FILENAME = "chapter6.mdl";
```

```
        public const string SAMPLE_DATA = "sampledata.csv";

        public const string TEST_DATA = "testdata.csv";
    }
}
```

The LoginHistory class

The LoginHistory class is the container class that contains the data to both predict and train our model. As described in previous chapters, the number in the LoadColumn decorator maps to the index in the CSV files. Each property maps to a value that will be sent into the model for anomaly detection:

```
using Microsoft.ML.Data;

namespace chapter06.ML.Objects
{
    public class LoginHistory
    {
        [LoadColumn(0)]
        public float UserID { get; set; }

        [LoadColumn(1)]
        public float CorporateNetwork { get; set; }

        [LoadColumn(2)]
        public float HomeNetwork { get; set; }

        [LoadColumn(3)]
        public float WithinWorkHours { get; set; }

        [LoadColumn(4)]
        public float WorkDay { get; set; }

        [LoadColumn(5)]
        public float Label { get; set; }
    }
}
```

The LoginPrediction class

The LoginPrediction class contains the properties mapped to our prediction output. The following PredictedLabel property will hold our prediction, while the Label and Score properties are used for evaluation:

```
namespace chapter06.ML.Objects
{
    public class LoginPrediction
    {
        public float Label;

        public float Score;

        public bool PredictedLabel;
    }
}
```

The Predictor class

There are a couple of changes to make to this class in order to handle the Login anomaly detection scenario:

1. First, we create our prediction engine with the LoginHistory and LoginPrediction types:

    ```
    var predictionEngine =
    MlContext.Model.CreatePredictionEngine<LoginHistory,
    LoginPrediction>(mlModel);
    ```

2. Next, we read the input file into a string variable:

    ```
    var json = File.ReadAllText(inputDataFile);
    ```

3. Lastly, we run the prediction and then output the results of the model run:

```
var prediction =
predictionEngine.Predict(JsonConvert.DeserializeObject<LoginHistory
>(json));

Console.WriteLine(
        $"Based on input json:{System.Environment.NewLine}" +
        $"{json}{System.Environment.NewLine}" +
        $"The login history is {
           (prediction.PredictedLabel ? "abnormal" : "normal")},
           with a {prediction.Score:F2} outlier score");
```

The Trainer class

Inside the `Trainer` class, several modifications need to be made to support anomaly detection classification using the randomized PCA trainer:

1. The first change is the addition of a `GetDataView` helper method, which builds the `IDataView` data view from the columns previously defined in the `LoginHistory` class:

```
private (IDataView DataView, IEstimator<ITransformer> Transformer)
GetDataView(string fileName, bool training = true)
{
    var trainingDataView =
MlContext.Data.LoadFromTextFile<LoginHistory>(fileName, ',');

    if (!training)
    {
        return (trainingDataView, null);
    }

    IEstimator<ITransformer> dataProcessPipeline =
            MlContext.Transforms.Concatenate(FEATURES,
               typeof(LoginHistory).ToPropertyList<LoginHistory>
                 (nameof(LoginHistory.Label)));

    return (trainingDataView, dataProcessPipeline);
}
```

2. We then build the training data view and the
`RandomizedPcaTrainer.Options` object:

```
var trainingDataView = GetDataView(trainingFileName);

var options = new RandomizedPcaTrainer.Options
{
    FeatureColumnName = FEATURES,
    ExampleWeightColumnName = null,
    Rank = 5,
    Oversampling = 20,
    EnsureZeroMean = true,
    Seed = 1
};
```

Note that the `Rank` property must be equal to or less than the features.

3. We can then create the randomized PCA trainer, append it to the training data view, fit our model, and then save it:

```
IEstimator<ITransformer> trainer =
MlContext.AnomalyDetection.Trainers.RandomizedPca(options:
options);

EstimatorChain<ITransformer> trainingPipeline =
trainingDataView.Transformer.Append(trainer);

TransformerChain<ITransformer> trainedModel =
trainingPipeline.Fit(trainingDataView.DataView);

MlContext.Model.Save(trainedModel,
trainingDataView.DataView.Schema, ModelPath);
```

4. Now we evaluate the model we just trained using the testing dataset:

```
var testingDataView = GetDataView(testingFileName, true);

var testSetTransform =
trainedModel.Transform(testingDataView.DataView);

var modelMetrics =
MlContext.AnomalyDetection.Evaluate(testSetTransform);
```

5. Finally, we output all of the classification metrics. Each of these will be detailed in the next section:

```
Console.WriteLine(
    $"Area Under Curve: {modelMetrics.AreaUnderRocCurve:P2}
                        {Environment.NewLine}" +
    $"Detection at FP Count:
        {modelMetrics.DetectionRateAtFalsePositiveCount}");
```

Running the application

To run the application, the process we use is nearly identical to Chapter 3, *Regression Model's* example application with the addition of passing in the test dataset when training:

1. After extracting data, we must train the model by passing in the newly created sampledata.csv and testdata.csv files:

```
PS chapter06\bin\Debug\netcoreapp3.0> .\chapter06.exe train
..\..\..\Data\sampledata.csv ..\..\..\Data\testdata.csv
Area Under Curve: 78.12%
Detection at FP Count: 1
```

2. To run the model with this file, simply pass in a constructed JSON file (input.json, in this case) and the predicted output will show:

```
PS chapter06\bin\Debug\netcoreapp3.0> .\chapter06.exe predict
input.json
Based on input json:
{
 "UserID": 0, "CorporateNetwork": 1, "HomeNetwork": 0,
"WithinWorkHours": 1, "WorkDay": 1
}
The login history is normal, with a 0% score
```

Note the expanded output of the model training to include two metric data points. We will go through what each one of these means at the end of this chapter.

Feel free to modify the values and explore how the prediction changes based on the dataset that the model was trained on. A few areas of experimentation from this point might include the following:

- Adding some additional properties to increase the prediction accuracy in a production scenario such as the hour of the day the login occurred
- Adding diversity to the training and test data

Evaluating a randomized PCA model

As discussed in previous chapters, evaluating a model is a critical part of the overall model-building process. A poorly trained model will only provide inaccurate predictions. Fortunately, ML.NET provides many popular attributes to calculate model accuracy based on a test set at the time of training to give you an idea of how well your model will perform in a production environment.

In ML.NET, as noted in the example application, there are two properties that comprise the `AnomalyDetectionMetrics` class object. Let's dive into the properties exposed in the `AnomalyDetectionMetrics` object:

- Area under the ROC curve
- Detection rate at false positive count

In the next sections, we will break down how these values are calculated and ideal values to look for.

Area under the ROC curve

The area under the ROC curve, as mentioned in `Chapter 3`, *Regression Model*, is, as the name implies, the area under the **Receiver Operating Characteristic (ROC)** curve. One question that might come to mind is this: how is this relevant to evaluating an anomaly detection model?

This computed area is equal to the chance that the algorithm, randomized PCA, in our case, scores a positive instance higher than a negative one, both chosen randomly to better evaluate the data. The number returned closer to 100% is the ideal value, while if it is closer to 0%, you will more than likely have significant false positives. You might remember our earlier example application getting 78%. This means that there was a 22% chance of a false positive; the following outlines some suggestions to improve the model and should reduce this number.

The following diagram visually reflects both a random guessing line and an arbitrary data curve. The area under the data curve in between the random guessing line is the area under the ROC curve data metric:

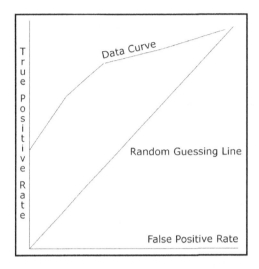

Detection rate at false positive count

The detection rate at false positive count property is the detection rate of K false positives. A false positive in an anomaly detection scenario would be to consider a data point an anomaly when, in fact, it was not. This rate is computed as follows:

Detection Rate of K False Positives = X / Y

Here, X is calculated to be the top test samples based on the scores previously described in the anomaly detection example (sorted in descending order). These are considered the top true positives (that is, more likely to be actual anomalies).

Y is calculated to be the total number of anomalies in the test data regardless of the score value (not filtering to points that look suspicious or not). In theory, this number could be very high if the number of false positives is high in your training data. As you build production models with randomized PCA, ensure your data represents as close to production as possible to avoid overfitting or underfitting to anomalies.

Summary

Over the course of this chapter, we discussed ML.NET's anomaly detection support via the randomized PCA algorithm. We also created and trained our first anomaly detection application using the randomized PCA algorithm to predict abnormal logins. In addition to this, we created a time series application, looking at network traffic and finding spikes in the amount of transferred data. Finally, we also looked at how to evaluate an anomaly detection model and the various properties that ML.NET exposes to achieve a proper evaluation of an anomaly detection model.

In the next chapter, we will deep dive into matrix factorization with ML.NET to create a music preference predictor.

Matrix Factorization Model

7

With anomaly detection models behind us, it is now time to dive into matrix factorization models. Matrix factorization is one of the newer additions to ML.NET, with a transform of the same name. In this chapter, we will dive into matrix factorization, as well as the various applications best suited to utilizing matrix factorization. In addition, we will build a new sample application to predict music recommendations based on the sample training data. Finally, we will explore how to evaluate a matrix factorization model with the properties that ML.NET exposes.

In this chapter, we will cover the following topics:

- Breaking down matrix factorizations
- Creating a matrix factorization application
- Evaluating a matrix factorization model

Breaking down matrix factorizations

As mentioned in Chapter 1, *Getting Started with Machine Learning and ML.NET*, matrix factorization, by definition, is an unsupervised learning algorithm. This means that the algorithm will train on data and build a matrix of patterns in user ratings, and during a prediction call, will attempt to find like ratings based on the data provided. In this section, we will dive into use cases for matrix factorization and have a look into the matrix factorization trainer in ML.NET.

Use cases for matrix factorizations

Matrix factorizations, as you might be starting to realize, have numerous applications where data is available, but the idea is to suggest other matches based on previously unselected data. Without needing to do manual spot-checking, matrix factorization algorithms train on this unselected data and determine patterns using a key-value pair combination. ML.NET provides various matrix factorization values to look at programmatically, inside of your application. We will review these values later on in this chapter, to better ensure the recommendation was not a false positive.

Some of the potential applications best suited for matrix factorization are:

- Music recommendations
- Product recommendations
- Movie recommendations
- Book recommendations

Effectively, anything where data can be traced back to a single user and then built upon as more data is entered can utilize matrix factorizations. This problem is called a **cold start problem**. Take, for instance, a new music platform geared toward helping you to find new bands to listen to. When you first reach the site and create a profile, there is no prior data available. You, as the end user, must tell the system what you like and don't like. Due to the nature of the algorithm, matrix factorization is better suited to this application than the straight regression or binary classification algorithms we explored in earlier chapters.

Diving into the matrix factorization trainer

The matrix factorization trainer is the only traditional trainer found in ML.NET as of this writing. The matrix factorization trainer requires both normalization of the values and caching. In addition, to utilize matrix factorization in ML.NET, the `Microsoft.ML.Recommender` NuGet package is required if you are creating the project from scratch. The included sample from the GitHub repository includes this package.

Similar to other algorithms, normalization is required, but matrix factorization is unique. Other algorithms, as we have seen with binary classification or regression algorithms, have multiple values that can be normalized. In matrix factorization, there are only three values involved: `Label`, `Row`, and `Column` values. The output is comprised of two properties: `Score` and `Label`. The `Score` value is of type `Float`, non-negative and unbounded.

It should be noted that in July 2018's ML.NET 0.3 update, field-aware factorization machines were added. However, this type of trainer offered only binary recommendations (such as either like or dislike), as opposed to matrix factorization, which supports floating-point values of any range. This provides considerably better flexibility in usage, such as getting more granular predictions. If, for instance, a matrix factorization recommendation on a scale from 0 to 100 returned 30, the recommendation engine would more than likely return a negative recommendation. With simply a binary response, the application—and thereby the end-user—is not shown how strong the recommendation is either way.

We will demonstrate this trainer in the sample application later, in the next section, by providing music recommendations.

Creating a matrix factorization application

As mentioned earlier, the application we will be creating is for music prediction. Given a UserID, MusicID, and a rating, the algorithm will use that data to create recommendations. As with other applications, this is not meant to power the next Spotifyesque machine learning product; however, it will show you how to use matrix factorization in ML.NET.

As with previous chapters, the completed project code, sample dataset, and project files can be downloaded here: `https://github.com/PacktPublishing/Hands-On-Machine-Learning-With-ML.NET/tree/master/chapter07`.

Exploring the project architecture

Building on the project architecture and code we created in previous chapters, the bulk of the changes are in the training of the model, as matrix factorization requires a fairly significant paradigm shift from what we have reviewed in previous chapters.

In the following screenshot, you will find the Visual Studio Solution Explorer view of the project. The new additions to the solution are the MusicRating and MusicPrediction files, which we will review later in this section:

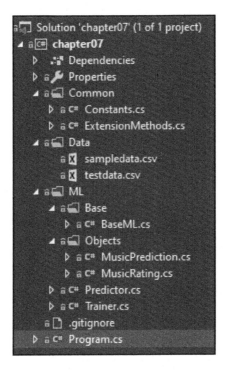

The sampledata.csv file contains 10 rows of random music ratings. Feel free to adjust the data to fit your own observations, or to adjust the trained model. Here is a snippet of the data:

```
1,1000,4
1,1001,3.5
1,1002,1
1,1003,2
2,1000,1.5
2,1001,2
2,1002,4
2,1003,4
3,1000,1
3,1001,3
```

Each of these rows contains the value for the properties in the newly created MusicRating class that we will review later on in this chapter.

In addition to this, we added the `testdata.csv` file that contains additional data points to test the newly trained model against and evaluate. Here is a snippet of the data inside of `testdata.csv`:

```
1,1000,4
1,1001,3.5
2,1002,1
2,1003,2
3,1000,1.5
3,1001,2
4,1002,4
4,1003,4
```

Diving into the code

For this application, as noted in the previous section, we are building on top of the work completed in Chapter 6, *Anomaly Detection Model*. For this deep dive, we are going to focus solely on the code that was changed for this application.

Classes that were changed or added are as follows:

- MusicRating
- MusicPrediction
- Predictor
- Trainer
- Constants

The MusicRating class

The `MusicRating` class is the container class that contains the data to both predict and train our model. As described in previous chapters, the number in the `LoadColumn` decorator maps to the index in the CSV files. As noted in the earlier section, matrix factorization in ML.NET requires the use of normalization, as shown in the following code block:

```
using Microsoft.ML.Data;

namespace chapter07.ML.Objects
{
    public class MusicRating
    {
        [LoadColumn(0)]
```

```
        public float UserID { get; set; }

        [LoadColumn(1)]
        public float MovieID { get; set; }

        [LoadColumn(2)]
        public float Label { get; set; }
    }
}
```

The MusicPrediction class

The MusicPrediction class contains the properties mapped to our prediction output. The Score contains the likelihood the prediction is accurate. We will review these values later on in this section, but for now, they can be seen in the following code block:

```
namespace chapter07.ML.Objects
{
    public class MusicPrediction
    {
        public float Label { get; set; }

        public float Score { get; set; }
    }
}
```

The Predictor class

There are a couple of changes in this class to handle the music-prediction scenario, as follows:

1. First, we create our prediction engine with the MusicRating and MusicPrediction types, like this:

   ```
   var predictionEngine =
   MlContext.Model.CreatePredictionEngine<MusicRating,
   MusicPrediction>(mlModel);
   ```

2. Next, we read the input file into a string object, like this:

   ```
   var json = File.ReadAllText(inputDataFile);
   ```

3. Next, we deserialize the string into an object of type `MusicRating`, like this:

```
var rating = JsonConvert.DeserializeObject<MusicRating>(json);
```

4. Lastly, we need to run the prediction, and then output the results of the model run, as follows:

```
var prediction = predictionEngine.Predict(rating);

Console.WriteLine(
    $"Based on input:{System.Environment.NewLine}" +
    $"Label: {rating.Label} | MusicID: {rating.MusicID} |
       UserID: {rating.UserID}{System.Environment.NewLine}" +
    $"The music is {(prediction.Score > Constants.SCORE_THRESHOLD ?
                    "recommended" : "not recommended")}");
```

With the transform only returning the three-element vector, the original row data is outputted to give context.

The Trainer class

Inside the `Trainer` class, several modifications need to be made to support the matrix factorization. In many ways, a simplification is required due to the nature of only having three inputs:

1. The first addition is the two constant variables for the variable encoding, shown in the following code block:

```
private const string UserIDEncoding = "UserIDEncoding";
private const string MovieIDEncoding = "MovieIDEncoding";
```

2. We then build the `MatrixFactorizationTrainer` options. The `Row` and `Column` properties are set to the column names previously defined. The `Quiet` flag displays additional model building information on every iteration, as illustrated in the following code block:

```
var options = new MatrixFactorizationTrainer.Options
{
    MatrixColumnIndexColumnName = UserIDEncoding,
    MatrixRowIndexColumnName = MovieIDEncoding,
    LabelColumnName = "Label",
    NumberOfIterations = 20,
    ApproximationRank = 10,
    Quiet = false
};
```

3. We can then create the matrix factorization trainer, as follows:

```
var trainingPipeline =
trainingDataView.Transformer.Append(MlContext.Recommendation().Trai
ners.MatrixFactorization(options));
```

4. Now, we fit the model on the training data and save the model, as follows:

```
ITransformer trainedModel =
trainingPipeLine.Fit(trainingDataView.DataView);

MlContext.Model.Save(trainedModel,
trainingDataView.DataView.Schema, ModelPath);

Console.WriteLine($"Model saved to
{ModelPath}{Environment.NewLine}");
```

5. Lastly, we load the testing data and pass the data to the matrix factorization evaluator, like this:

```
var testingDataView = GetDataView(testingFileName, true);

var testSetTransform =
trainedModel.Transform(testingDataView.DataView);

var modelMetrics =
MlContext.Recommendation().Evaluate(testSetTransform);

Console.WriteLine(
        $"matrix factorization Evaluation:{Environment.NewLine}
                        {Environment.NewLine}" +
        $"Loss Function: {modelMetrics.LossFunction}
                        {Environment.NewLine}" +
        $"Mean Absolute Error: {modelMetrics.MeanAbsoluteError}
                        {Environment.NewLine}" +
        $"Mean Squared Error: {modelMetrics.MeanSquaredError}
                        {Environment.NewLine}" +
        $"R Squared: {modelMetrics.RSquared}{Environment.NewLine}"+
        $"Root Mean Squared Error:
                        {modelMetrics.RootMeanSquaredError}");
```

The Constants class

In addition, given the training only requires the training data, some modifications to the `Program` class need to be performed, as follows:

```
namespace chapter07.Common
{
    public class Constants
    {
        public const string MODEL_FILENAME = "chapter7.mdl";

        public const float SCORE_THRESHOLD = 3.0f;
    }
}
```

Running the application

To run the application, the process is nearly identical to Chapter 6's sample application, as follows:

1. After preparing the data, we must then train the model by passing in the newly created `sampledata.csv` file, like this:

```
PS Debug\netcoreapp3.0> .\chapter07.exe train
..\..\..\Data\sampledata.csv ..\..\..\Data\testdata.csv
iter tr_rmse obj
   0 2.4172 9.6129e+01
   1 1.9634 6.6078e+01
   2 1.5140 4.2233e+01
   3 1.3417 3.5027e+01
   4 1.2860 3.2934e+01
   5 1.1818 2.9107e+01
   6 1.1414 2.7737e+01
   7 1.0669 2.4966e+01
   8 0.9819 2.2615e+01
   9 0.9055 2.0387e+01
  10 0.8656 1.9472e+01
  11 0.7534 1.6725e+01
  12 0.6862 1.5413e+01
  13 0.6240 1.4311e+01
  14 0.5621 1.3231e+01
  15 0.5241 1.2795e+01
  16 0.4863 1.2281e+01
  17 0.4571 1.1938e+01
```

```
18 0.4209 1.1532e+01
19 0.3975 1.1227e+01
```

```
Model saved to Debug\netcoreapp3.0\chapter7.mdl
```

2. To run the model with this file, simply pass the `testdata.csv` file mentioned earlier into the newly built application, and the predicted output will show the following:

```
matrix factorization Evaluation:

Loss Function: 0.140
Mean Absolute Error: 0.279
Mean Squared Error: 0.140
R Squared: 0.922
Root Mean Squared Error: 0.375
```

Prior to running the prediction, create a JSON file in Notepad with the following text:

```
{ "UserID": 10, "MusicID": 4, "Label": 3 }
```

Then save the file to your output folder.

3. Then, run the prediction, like this:

```
PS Debug\netcoreapp3.0> .\chapter07.exe predict input.json
Based on input:
Label: 3 | MusicID: 4 | UserID: 10
The music is not recommended
```

Feel free to modify the values, and see how the prediction changes based on the dataset that the model was trained on. A few areas of experimentation from this point might be to:

- Change the hyperparameters mentioned in the `Trainer` class deep dive.
- Add diversification and more data points to the training and test data.

Evaluating a matrix factorization model

As discussed in previous chapters, evaluating a model is a critical part of the overall model-building process. A poorly trained model will only provide inaccurate predictions. Fortunately, ML.NET provides many popular attributes to calculate model accuracy based on a test set at the time of training, to give you an idea of how well your model will perform in a production environment.

As noted earlier in the sample application, for matrix factorization model evaluation in ML.NET, there are five properties that comprise the `RegressionMetrics` class object. Let us dive into the properties exposed in the `RegressionMetrics` object here:

- Loss function
- **Mean Squared Error (MSE)**
- **Mean Absolute Error (MAE)**
- R-squared
- **Root Mean Squared Error (RMSE)**

In the next sections, we will break down how these values are calculated, and detail the ideal values to look for.

Loss function

This property uses the loss function set when the matrix factorization trainer was initialized. In the case of our matrix factorization example application, we used the default constructor, which defaults to the `SquaredLossRegression` class.

Other regression loss functions offered by ML.NET are:

- Squared-loss one class
- Squared-loss regression

The idea behind this property is to allow some flexibility when it comes to evaluating your model compared to the other four properties, which use fixed algorithms for evaluation.

MSE

MSE is defined as the measure of the average of the squares of the errors. To put this simply, take the plot shown in the following screenshot:

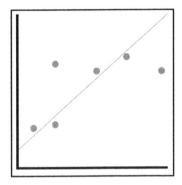

The dots correlate to data points for our model, while the line going across is the prediction line. The distance between the dots and the prediction line is the error. For MSE, the value is calculated based on these points and their distances to the line. From that value, the mean is calculated. For MSE, the smaller the value, the better the fitting, and the more accurate the predictions you will have with your model.

MSE is best used to evaluate models when outliers are critical to the prediction output.

MAE

MAE is similar to MSE, with the critical difference being that it sums the distances between the points and the prediction lines, as opposed to computing the mean. It should be noted that MAE does not take into account directions in calculating the sum. For instance, if you had two data points equal distance from the line, one above and the other below, in effect this would be balanced out with a positive and negative value. In machine learning, this is referred to as **Mean Bias Error** (**MBE**). However, ML.NET does not provide this as part of the `RegressionMetrics` class at the time of this writing.

MAE is best used to evaluate models when outliers are considered simply anomalies, and shouldn't be counted in evaluating a model's performance.

R-squared

R-squared, also called **the coefficient of determination**, is another method of representing how well the prediction compares to the test set. R-squared is calculated by taking the difference between each predicted value and its corresponding actual value, squaring that difference, then summing the squares for each pair of points.

R-squared values generally range between 0 and 1, represented as a floating-point value. A negative value can occur when the fitted model is evaluated to be worse than an average fit. However, a low number does not always reflect that the model is bad. Predictions, such as the one we looked at in this chapter, that are based on predicting human actions are often found to be under 50%.

Conversely, higher values aren't necessarily a sure sign of the model's performance, as this could be considered as overfitting of the model. This happens in cases when there are a lot of features fed to the model, thereby making the model more complex as compared to the model we built in the *Creating your first ML.NET application* section of Chapter 2, *Setting Up the ML.NET Environment*, as there is simply not enough diversity in the training and test sets. For example, if all of the employees were roughly the same values, and then the test set holdout was comprised of the same ranges of values, this would be considered overfitting.

RMSE

RMSE is arguably the easiest property to understand, given the previous methods. Take the plot shown in the following screenshot:

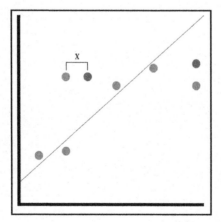

In the case of testing the model, as we did previously with the holdout set, the lighter dots are the actual values from the test set, while the darker dots are the predicted values. The **X** depicted is the distance between the predicted and actual values. RMSE simply takes a mean of all of those distances, squares that value, and then takes the square root.

A value under 180 is generally considered a good model.

Summary

Over the course of this chapter, we have deep-dived into ML.NET's matrix factorization support. We have also created and trained our first matrix factorization application to predict music recommendations. Lastly, we also dove into how to evaluate a matrix factorization model and looked at the various properties that ML.NET exposes to achieve a proper evaluation of a matrix factorization model.

With this chapter coming to a close, we have also completed our initial investigation of the various models ML.NET provides. In the next chapter, we will be creating full applications, building on the knowledge garnered over the last few chapters, with the first being a full .NET Core application providing stock forecasting.

Section 3: Real-World Integrations with ML.NET

3

This section deep dives into complete applications using the knowledge garnered in Section 2, *ML.NET Models*, for creating a console application in .NET Core, a web application, and a Windows 10 desktop application.

This section comprises the following chapters:

- Chapter 8, *Using ML.NET with .NET Core and Forecasting*
- Chapter 9, *Using ML.NET with ASP.NET Core*
- Chapter 10, *Using ML.NET with UWP*

8
Using ML.NET with .NET Core and Forecasting

Now that we have completed our deep dive into the various groups of algorithms ML.NET offers, we will begin to explore integrating ML.NET into a production application over the next few chapters. In this chapter, we will deep dive into a .NET Core console application building on the structure defined in previous chapters with a focus on hardening and error handling. The application we will be building uses forecasting to predict stock prices based on a series of trends. By the end of this chapter, you should have a firm grasp of designing and coding a production-grade .NET Core application with ML.NET.

In this chapter, we will cover the following topics:

- Breaking down the .NET Core application architecture
- Creating the forecasting application
- Exploring additional production application enhancements

Breaking down the .NET Core application architecture

As mentioned in Chapter 1, *Getting Started with Machine Learning and ML.NET*, .NET Core 3.x is the preferred platform for using ML.NET due to the optimization done in the 3.0 release. In addition, .NET Core provides a singular coding framework to target Linux, macOS, and Windows, as noted in the following diagram:

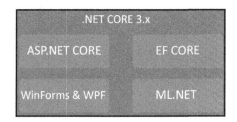

.NET Core architecture

From its inception in 2016, the underlying goals of .NET Core have been to provide rapid updates and feature parity with (the previously Windows-only) Microsoft .NET Framework. Over time and versions, the gap has gotten smaller by simply adding the APIs that were missing, using additional NuGet packages. One such example of this is Microsoft.Windows.Compatibility that provides 20,000 APIs not found in the Core framework including registry access, drawing, and Windows Permission Model access. This approach keeps the framework light and cross-platform but does introduce some design patterns to help you to develop your platform-specific applications.

Take, for instance, a Windows Desktop application that uses ML.NET to provide an **Intrusion Detection System (IDS)**. A simple approach would be to write all of the code in a .NET Core **Windows Presentation Foundation (WPF)** application. However, this would tie you to Windows only without doing major refactoring. A better approach would be to create a .NET Core class library that contains all platform-agnostic code and then creates abstract classes or interfaces to implement the platform-specific code inside your platform application.

.NET Core targets

As mentioned previously, .NET Core offers a single framework to target Windows, macOS, and Linux. However, this doesn't just apply to console applications as we have used throughout this book. Recent work in .NET Core 3 has provided the ability to port existing .NET Framework WPF and Windows Forms applications to .NET Core 3, thereby enabling applications that rely on potentially years-old frameworks to use the latest .NET Core advancements. In addition, web applications that previously used ASP.NET can be migrated over to ASP.NET Core (ASP.NET WebForms does not currently have a migration path).

Another benefit of .NET Core targeting is the ability to compile with the `--self-contained` flag. This flag compiles your application or library and then bundles all necessary .NET Core framework files. This allows you to deploy your application without a .NET prerequisite during install. This does make your overall build output larger, but in a customer scenario, a ~100MB increase far outweighs the deployment hurdles of prerequisites.

.NET Core future

You might wonder what the future of .NET Framework, Mono, and .NET Core is. Fortunately, Microsoft, at the time of this writing, has confirmed that all existing frameworks will be migrated into a singular framework simply called .NET 5. Previously, when making a decision on which framework to use, certain trade-offs were guaranteed. Hence, taking the benefits of each framework and unifying them for the first time will eliminate these trade-offs entirely. Take, for instance, Mono's **Ahead-Of-Time (AOT)** compilation or Xamarin's cross-platform UI support, which can be utilized inside an existing .NET Core 3.x application based on the information released.

A preview of .NET 5 is expected in the first half of 2020, with a production release in November 2020.

Creating the stock price estimator application

As mentioned earlier, the application we will be creating is a stock price estimator. Given a set of stock prices across days, weeks, or years, the forecasting algorithm will internally identify trending patterns. Unlike previous chapters, the application will be architected to be plugged into a production pipeline.

As with previous chapters, the completed project code, sample dataset, and project files can be downloaded from: `https://github.com/PacktPublishing/Hands-On-Machine-Learning-With-ML.NET/tree/master/chapter08`.

Exploring the project architecture

Building upon the project architecture and code we created in previous chapters, the architecture we will be exploring in this chapter further enhances the architecture to be more structured and thereby more usable for an end user.

Like in some of the previous chapters, an additional NuGet package—`Microsoft.ML.TimeSeries`—is required to utilize the forecasting functionality in ML.NET. Version 1.3.1 is used in both the included example on GitHub and throughout this chapter's deep dive.

In the following screenshot, you will find the Visual Studio Solution Explorer view of the project. There are several new additions to the solution to facilitate the production use case we are targeting. We will review in detail each of the new files shown in the solution screenshot here later on in this chapter:

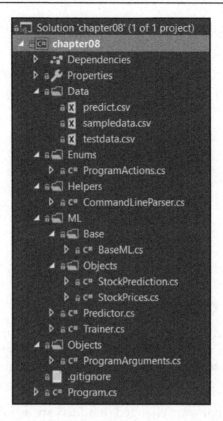

The `sampledata.csv` file contains 24 rows of stock prices. Feel free to adjust the data to fit your own observations or to adjust the trained model. Here is a snippet of the data:

```
33
34
301
33
44
299
40
50
400
60
76
500
```

Each of these rows contains the stock price value we will populate into a `StockPrices` class object that we will review later on in this chapter.

In addition to this, we added the `testdata.csv` file that contains additional data points to test the newly trained model against and evaluate it. Here is a snippet of the data inside of `testdata.csv`:

```
10
25
444
9
11
333
4
3
500
```

Diving into the code

For this application, as noted in the previous section, we are building on top of the work completed in previous chapters. However, for this chapter, we will be changing every file to support production use cases. For each file changed from previous chapters, we will review the changes made and the reasoning behind these changes.

Classes and enumerations that were changed or added are as follows:

- `ProgramActions`
- `CommandLineParser`
- `BaseML`
- `StockPrediction`
- `StockPrices`
- `Predictor`
- `Trainer`
- `ProgramArguments`
- `Program`

The ProgramActions enumeration

The following `ProgramActions` enumeration has been added to the solution to facilitate the use of a strongly typed and structured path for handling various actions the program performs:

```
namespace chapter08.Enums
{
    public enum ProgramActions
    {
        TRAINING,
        PREDICT
    }
}
```

In the case of this application, we only have two actions—`Training` and `Predicting`. However, as shown in previous chapters, you might also have a feature extraction step or maybe provide an evaluation step. This design pattern allows flexibility while also removing the **magic strings** problem mentioned at the beginning of this chapter.

The CommandLineParser class

The `CommandLineParser` class provides a program-agnostic parser for handling command-line arguments. In previous chapters, we were manually parsing the indexes and mapping those values to arguments. On the other hand, this approach creates a flexible, easy-to-maintain and structured response object that maps arguments directly to the properties. Let's now dive into the class:

1. First, we define the function prototype:

```
public static T ParseArguments<T>(string[] args)
```

   The use of generics (that is, `T`) creates a flexible approach to making this method unconstrained to just this application.

2. Next, we test for `null` arguments:

```
if (args == null)
{
    throw new ArgumentNullException(nameof(args));
}
```

3. Then, we test for empty arguments and let the user know default values are going to be used instead of failing, as in previous chapters:

```
if (args.Length == 0)
{
    Console.WriteLine("No arguments passed in - using defaults");

    return Activator.CreateInstance<T>();
}
```

4. After null and empty checks are performed, we then perform a multiple of two checks since all arguments are pairs:

```
if (args.Length % 2 != 0)
{
    throw new ArgumentException($"Arguments must be in pairs, there
were {args.Length} passed in");
}
```

5. Continuing, we then create an object of the `T` type using the `Activator.CreateInstance` method:

```
var argumentObject = Activator.CreateInstance<T>();
```

Ensure that, when creating class objects, the constructor has no arguments as this call would throw an exception if so. If you create an object with constructor parameters and without a parameterless constructor, use the overload of `Activator.CreateInstance` and pass in the required parameters.

6. Next, we utilize reflection to grab all of the properties of the `T` type:

```
var properties = argumentObject.GetType().GetProperties();
```

7. Now that we have both the generic object created and the properties of that object, we then loop through each of the argument key/value pairs and set the property in the object:

```
for (var x = 0; x < args.Length; x += 2)
{
    var property = properties.FirstOrDefault(
                a => a.Name.Equals(args[x],
                StringComparison.CurrentCultureIgnoreCase));

    if (property == null)
    {
        Console.WriteLine($"{args[x]} is an invalid argument");
```

```
                continue;
        }

        if (property.PropertyType.IsEnum)
        {
            property.SetValue(argumentObject,
                            Enum.Parse(property.PropertyType,
                            args[x + 1], true));
        }
        else
        {
            property.SetValue(argumentObject, args[x + 1]);
        }
    }
```

Note the special case for the IsEnum function to handle our previously covered
ProgramActions enumeration. Since a string value cannot be automatically converted to
an enumeration, we needed to handle the string-to-enumeration conversion specifically
with the Enum.Parse method. As written, the enumeration handler is generic if you add
more enumerations to the T type.

The BaseML class

The BaseML class for this application has been streamlined to simply instantiate the
MLContext object:

```
using Microsoft.ML;

namespace chapter08.ML.Base
{
    public class BaseML
    {
        protected readonly MLContext MlContext;

        protected BaseML()
        {
            MlContext = new MLContext(2020);
        }
    }
}
```

The StockPrediction class

The `StockPrediction` class is the container for our prediction values, as defined here:

```
namespace chapter08.ML.Objects
{
    public class StockPrediction
    {
        public float[] StockForecast { get; set; }

        public float[] LowerBound { get; set; }

        public float[] UpperBound { get; set; }
    }
}
```

The `StockForecast` property will hold our predicted stock values based on the model training and submitted value to the prediction engine. The `LowerBound` and `UpperBound` values hold the lowest and highest estimated values respectively.

The StockPrices class

The `StockPrices` class contains our single floating-point value holding the stock price. To keep the code cleaner when populating the values, a constructor accepting the stock price value has been added:

```
using Microsoft.ML.Data;

namespace chapter08.ML.Objects
{
    public class StockPrices
    {
        [LoadColumn(0)]
        public float StockPrice;

        public StockPrices(float stockPrice)
        {
            StockPrice = stockPrice;
        }
    }
}
```

The Predictor class

The `Predictor` class, in comparison to previous chapters, has been streamlined and adapted to support forecasting:

1. First, we adjust the `Predict` method to accept the newly defined `ProgramArguments` class object:

```
public void Predict(ProgramArguments arguments)
```

2. Next, we update the model `file.Exists` check to utilize the `arguments` object:

```
if (!File.Exists(arguments.ModelFileName))
{
    Console.WriteLine(
        $"Failed to find model at {arguments.ModelFileName}");

    return;
}
```

3. Similarly, we also update the prediction filename reference to the utilize the `arguments` object:

```
if (!File.Exists(arguments.PredictionFileName))
{
    Console.WriteLine(
        $"Failed to find input data at {
                        arguments.PredictionFileName}");

    return;
}
```

4. Next, we also modify the model open call to utilize the `arguments` object:

```
using (var stream = new
FileStream(Path.Combine(AppContext.BaseDirectory,
arguments.ModelFileName), FileMode.Open, FileAccess.Read,
FileShare.Read))
{
    mlModel = MlContext.Model.Load(stream, out _);
}
```

5. We then create the Time Series Engine object with our `StockPrices` and `StockPrediction` types:

    ```
    var predictionEngine = mlModel.CreateTimeSeriesEngine<StockPrices,
    StockPrediction>(MlContext);
    ```

6. Next, we read the stock price prediction file into a string array:

    ```
    var stockPrices = File.ReadAllLines(arguments.PredictionFileName);
    ```

7. Lastly, we iterate through each input, call the prediction engine, and display the estimated values:

    ```
    foreach (var stockPrice in stockPrices)
    {
        var prediction = predictionEngine.Predict(
                    new StockPrices(Convert.ToSingle(stockPrice)));

        Console.WriteLine(
                $"Given a stock price of ${stockPrice},
                        the next 5 values are predicted to be: " +
                $"{string.Join(", ", prediction.StockForecast.Select(
                        a => $"${Math.Round(a)}"))}");
    }
    ```

The Trainer class

The `Trainer` class, akin to the `Predictor` class, received both streamlining and changes to account for the ML.NET forecasting algorithm:

1. First, update the function prototype to take the `ProgramArguments` object:

    ```
    public void Train(ProgramArguments arguments)
    ```

2. Next, we update the training file check to utilize the `argument` object:

    ```
    if (!File.Exists(arguments.TrainingFileName))
    {
        Console.WriteLine($"Failed to find training data file
    ({arguments.TrainingFileName})");

        return;
    }
    ```

3. Similarly, we then update the testing file check to utilize the `argument` object:

```
if (!File.Exists(arguments.TestingFileName))
{
    Console.WriteLine($"Failed to find test data file
                    ({arguments.TestingFileName})");

    return;
}
```

4. Next, we load the `StockPrices` values from the training file:

```
var dataView =
MlContext.Data.LoadFromTextFile<StockPrices>(arguments.TrainingFile
Name);
```

5. We then create the `Forecasting` object and utilize the `nameof` C# feature to avoid magic string references:

```
var model = MlContext.Forecasting.ForecastBySsa(
    outputColumnName: nameof(StockPrediction.StockForecast),
    inputColumnName: nameof(StockPrices.StockPrice),
    windowSize: 7,
    seriesLength: 30,
    trainSize: 24,
    horizon: 5,
    confidenceLevel: 0.95f,
    confidenceLowerBoundColumn: nameof(StockPrediction.LowerBound),
    confidenceUpperBoundColumn: nameof(StockPrediction.UpperBound));
```

The input and output column name references are as we have seen in previous chapters. The `windowSize` property is the duration between the data points in the training set. For this application, we are using 7 to indicate a week's duration. The `seriesLength` property indicates the total duration of the dataset in this case. The `horizon` property indicates how many predicted values should be calculated when the model is run. In our case, we are asking for 5 predicted values.

6. Lastly, we transform the model with the training data, call the `CreateTimeSeriesEngine` method, and write the model to disk:

```
var transformer = model.Fit(dataView);

var forecastEngine =
transformer.CreateTimeSeriesEngine<StockPrices,
StockPrediction>(MlContext);

forecastEngine.CheckPoint(MlContext, arguments.ModelFileName);

Console.WriteLine($"Wrote model to {arguments.ModelFileName}");
```

The ProgramArguments class

This new class, as referred to earlier in this section, provides the one-to-one mapping of arguments to properties used throughout the application:

1. First, we define the properties that map directly to the command-line arguments:

```
public ProgramActions Action { get; set; }

public string TrainingFileName { get; set; }

public string TestingFileName { get; set; }

public string PredictionFileName { get; set; }

public string ModelFileName { get; set; }
```

2. Lastly, we populate default values for the properties:

```
public ProgramArguments()
{
    ModelFileName = "chapter8.mdl";

    PredictionFileName = @"..\..\..\Data\predict.csv";

    TrainingFileName = @"..\..\..\Data\sampledata.csv";

    TestingFileName = @"..\..\..\Data\testdata.csv";
}
```

Unlike previous chapters, if any property was not set as expected, the program would fail. This is fine for the developer experience; however, in the real world, end users will more than likely attempt to just run the application without any parameters.

The Program class

Inside the `Program` class, the code has been simplified to utilize the new `CommandLineParser` class discussed earlier in this chapter. With the use of the `CommandLineParser` class, all of the actions have been switched to utilize strongly-typed enumerations:

1. First, while relatively simplistic, clearing the screen of any previous run data is an improved UX:

   ```
   Console.Clear();
   ```

2. We then use our new `CommandLineParser` class and associated `ParseArguments` method to create a strongly-typed argument object:

   ```
   var arguments =
   CommandLineParser.ParseArguments<ProgramArguments>(args);
   ```

3. We then can use a simplified and strongly typed switch case to handle our two actions:

   ```
   switch (arguments.Action)
   {
       case ProgramActions.PREDICT:
           new Predictor().Predict(arguments);
           break;
       case ProgramActions.TRAINING:
           new Trainer().Train(arguments);
           break;
       default:
           Console.WriteLine($"Unhandled action {arguments.Action}");
           break;
   }
   ```

Running the application

To run the application, the process is nearly identical to the sample application in Chapter 3, *Regression Model*, with the addition of passing in the test dataset when training:

1. Running the application without any arguments to train the model, we use the following step:

   ```
   PS chapter08\bin\Debug\netcoreapp3.0> .\chapter08.exe
   No arguments passed in - using defaults
   Wrote model to chapter8.mdl
   ```

2. Running the application to make predicitons based on the included prediction data, we use the following step:

   ```
   PS chapter08\bin\Debug\netcoreapp3.0> .\chapter08.exe action
   predict
   Given a stock price of $101, the next 5 values are predicted to be:
   $128, $925, $140, $145, $1057
   Given a stock price of $102, the next 5 values are predicted to be:
   $924, $138, $136, $1057, $158
   Given a stock price of $300, the next 5 values are predicted to be:
   $136, $134, $852, $156, $150
   Given a stock price of $40, the next 5 values are predicted to be:
   $133, $795, $122, $149, $864
   Given a stock price of $30, the next 5 values are predicted to be:
   $767, $111, $114, $837, $122
   Given a stock price of $400, the next 5 values are predicted to be:
   $105, $102, $676, $116, $108
   Given a stock price of $55, the next 5 values are predicted to be:
   $97, $594, $91, $103, $645
   Given a stock price of $69, the next 5 values are predicted to be:
   $557, $81, $87, $605, $90
   Given a stock price of $430, the next 5 values are predicted to be:
   $76, $78, $515, $84, $85
   ```

Feel free to modify the values and see how the prediction changes based on the dataset that the model was trained on. A few areas of experimentation from this point might be to do the following:

- Tweak the hyperparameters reviewed in the Trainer class, such as the windowSize, seriesLength, or horizon properties, to see how accuracy is affected.
- Add significantly more data points—this may utilize a data feed of your favorite stock you watch.

Exploring additional production application enhancements

Now that we have completed our deep dive, there are a couple of additional elements to possibly further enhance the application. A few ideas are discussed here.

Logging

Logging utilizing NLog (`https://nlog-project.org/`) or a similar open source project is highly recommended as your application complexity increases. This will allow you to log to a file, console, or third-party logging solution such as Loggly at varying levels. For instance, if you deploy this application to a customer, breaking down the error level to at least Debug, Warning, and Error will be helpful when debugging issues remotely.

Utilizing Reflection further

As noted earlier in this section to create flexibility and adaptability, we utilized `Reflection` to parse the command-line arguments. You could take this a step further and replace the switch case statement/standard flow in the `Program` class with an entirely reflection-based approach, meaning for every action defined in the application, it could inherit from an abstract `BaseAction` class and at runtime, based on the argument, call the appropriate class. For every new action, simply adding a new entry to the `ProgramActions` enumeration and then defining a class with that enumeration would be all that is required.

Utilizing a database

In a real-world scenario, the data provided to run predictions will more than likely come from a database. This database, whether it is a Postgres, SQL Server, or SQLite database (to name a few), can be accessed with Microsoft's Entity Framework Core or with ML.NET's built-in database loader method—`CreateDatabaseLoader`. This loader is akin to how we have loaded data from enumerable or text files with the extra steps of injecting SQL queries.

In a production scenario, given Entity Framework Core's performance and ability to use LINQ instead of plaintext over ML.NET's implementation (at the time of this writing), I would recommend using Entity Framework if database sources are utilized.

Summary

Throughout this chapter, we have deep-dived into what goes into a production-ready .NET Core application architecture using the work performed in previous chapters as a foundation. We also created a brand new stock price estimator using the forecasting algorithm in ML.NET. Lastly, we discussed some ways to further enhance a .NET Core application (and production applications in general).

In the next chapter, we will deep dive into creating a production-file-classification web application using ML.NET's binary classification and ASP.NET Core's framework.

Using ML.NET with ASP.NET Core

9

Now that we have an idea of how to create a production-grade .NET Core console application, in this chapter, we will deep dive into creating a fully functional ASP.NET Core Blazor web application. This application will utilize an ML.NET binary classification model to make file classifications on Windows executables (**Portable Executable (PE)** files), in order to determine whether the files themselves are either clean or malicious. Furthermore, we will explore breaking our application code into a component-based architecture using a .NET Core library to share between our web application and the console application that will train our model. By the end of the chapter, you should have a firm grasp of designing and coding a production-grade ASP.NET Core Blazor web application with ML.NET.

In this chapter, we will cover the following topics:

- Breaking down ASP.NET Core
- Creating the file classification web application
- Exploring additional production-application enhancements

Breaking down ASP.NET Core

Building on the same .NET Core technology discussed in `Chapter 8`, *Using ML.NET with .NET Core and Forecasting*, ASP.NET Core adds a powerful web framework. This web framework includes a powerful rendering engine, Razor, in addition to supporting scalable **representational state transfer (REST)** services. The example in this chapter will use this technology to create our file classification frontend. In the next two sections, we will dive into the ASP.NET Core architecture and discuss Blazor, the new web framework from Microsoft.

Understanding the ASP.NET Core architecture

At a high level, ASP.NET Core builds on top of .NET Core, providing a fully-featured web framework. As with .NET Core, ASP.NET Core runs on Windows, Linux, and macOS, in addition to allowing deployments to x86, x64, and **Advanced RISC Machine (ARM)** CPU architectures.

A typical ASP.NET Core application includes the following:

- Models
- Views
- Controllers

These components form a common web architecture principle of **Model-View-Controller**, otherwise known as **MVC**.

Controllers

Controllers provide the server-side code for handling business logic for both web applications and REST services. Controllers can include both web and REST calls in the same controller, although I would recommend keeping them separate to ensure your code is organized cleanly.

Models

Models provide the container of data from the Controller to the View, and vice versa. For example, take a listing page pulling data from a database. The controller would return a model populated with that data, and if that same data was then used for filtering, it would also be serialized into **JavaScript Object Notation (JSON)** and sent back to the Controller.

Views

Views provide the templates for the frontend view with support for model binding. Model binding allows properties bound to various **Domain Object Model (DOM)** objects—such as textboxes, checkboxes, and dropdowns—to be cleanly mapped to and from. This approach of model binding has the added benefit of supporting strongly typed references, which comes in extremely handy when you have a complex View with dozens of properties bound to a Model.

Form handling with the model binding provides a similar model to the **Model-View ViewModel (MVVM)** approach we are going to dive into in `Chapter 10`, *Using ML.NET with UWP*, with a **Universal Windows Platform (UWP)** application.

> If you want to deep dive further into ASP.NET, Channel 9 from Microsoft has a series called ASP.NET Core 101 that covers all of the main aspects of ASP.NET, at `https://channel9.msdn.com/Series/ASPNET-Core-101`.

Blazor

Building on the ASP.NET Core infrastructure, Blazor focuses on removing one of the biggest hurdles with complex web applications—**JavaScript**. Blazor allows you to write C# code instead of JavaScript code to handle client-side tasks such as form handling, HTTP calls, and asynchronously loading data. Under the hood, Blazor uses **WebAssembly (Wasm)**, a popular high-performant JavaScript framework supported by all current browsers (Edge, Safari, Chrome, and Firefox).

Similar to other frameworks, Blazor also supports and recommends the use of modular components to promote reuse. These are called **Blazor components**.

In addition, there are three project types when creating a Blazor application:

- The Blazor-only client side is used, which is ideal for more static pages.
- A Blazor (ASP.NET Core-hosted) client-side application that is hosted inside ASP.NET Core (this is the project type we are going to review in the next section).
- A Blazor server-side application that updates the DOM. This is ideal for use with SignalR, Microsoft's real-time web framework supporting chats, real-time tickers, and maps, to name but a few.

> If you want to deep dive further into Blazor, Microsoft has written an abundant amount of documentation on **Microsoft Developer Network (MSDN)** at: `https://docs.microsoft.com/en-us/aspnet/core/blazor/?view=aspnetcore-3.1`.

Creating the file classification web application

As mentioned earlier, the application we will be creating is a file classification web application. Using the knowledge garnered in the *Creating a binary classification application* section in Chapter 4, *Classification Model*, we will be taking it a step further and looking at adding more attributes to a file prior to making a classification. In addition, we will be integrating machine learning with ML.NET into the web application, where an end user can upload files for classification, returning either clean or malicious files, along with a confidence of that prediction.

As with previous chapters, the completed project code, sample dataset, and project files can be downloaded at: https://github.com/PacktPublishing/Hands-On-Machine-Learning-With-ML.NET/tree/master/chapter09.

Exploring the project architecture

Given the previous applications have all been command-line applications, the project architecture for this example is quite different.

As with some of the previous chapters, an additional ML.NET NuGet package—Microsoft.ML.FastTree—is required in order to utilize the FastTree algorithm in ML.NET. Version 1.3.1 is used in both the included example on GitHub and throughout this chapter's deep dive.

In the following screenshot, you will find the Visual Studio Solution Explorer view of the example's solution. Given that this example comprises three separate projects (more akin to a production scenario), the amount of both new and significantly modified files is quite large. We will review each of the new files shown in the following solution screenshot in detail in further sections:

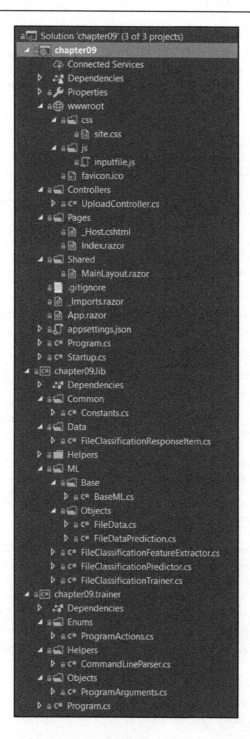

The `sampledata.csv` file contains 14 rows of extracted features from Windows Executables (we will go into these features in more detail in the next section). Feel free to adjust the data to fit your own observations or to adjust the trained model with different sample files. The following snippet is one of the rows found in the `sampledata.data` file:

```
18944 0 7 0 0 4 True "!This program cannot be run in DOS mode.Fm;Ld
&~_New_ptrt(M4_Alloc_max"uJIif94H3"j?TjV*?invalid argum_~9%sC:\Program
Files (x86\Microsoft Visu Studio\20cl4e\xomory"/Owneby CWGnkno excepti &
0xFF;b?eCErr[E7XE#D%d3kRegO(q/}nKeyExWa!0 S=+,H}Vo\DebugPE.pdbC,j?_info
ByteToWidendled=aekQ3V?$buic_g(@1@A8?5/wQAEAAV0;AH@Z?flush@Co12@XcCd{(kIN<7
BED!?rdbufPA[Tght_tDB.0J608(:6<?xml version='1.0' encoding='UTF8'
standalone='yes'?><assembly xmlns='urn:schemasmicrosoftcom:asm.v1'
manifestVersion='1.0'> <trustInfo xmlns="urn:schemasmicrosoftcom:asm.v3">
<security> <requestedPrivileges> <requestedExecutionLevel level='asInvoker'
uiAccess='false' /> </requestedPrivileges> </security>
</trustInfo></assembly>KERNEL32.DLLMSVCP140D.dllucrtbased.dllVCRUNTIME140D.
dllExitProcessGetProcAddressLoadLibraryAVirtualProtect??1_Lockit@std@@QAE@X
Z"
```

In addition to this, we added the `testdata.data` file that contains additional data points to test the newly trained model against and evaluate it. Here is a sample row of the data inside of `testdata.data`:

```
1670144 1 738 0 0 24 False "!This program cannot be run in DOS
mode.WATAUAVAWH A_AA]A\_t$ UWAVHx
UATAUAVAWHA_AA]A\]UVWATAUAVAWH|$@H!t$0HA_AA]A\_]VWATAVAWHSUVWATAUAVAWH(A_AA
]A\_][@USVWATAVAWHA_AA\_[]UVWATAUAVAWHA_AA]A\_]@USVWAVH` UAUAVHWATAUAVAWH
A_AA]A\_x ATAVAWHUSVWATAUAVAWHA_AA]A\_[]UVWATAUAVAWHA_AA]A\_]\$
UVWATAUAVAWHA_AA]A\_]x
UATAUAVAWHA_AA]A\]@USVWAVHUVWATAUAVAWHA_AA]A\_]UVWATAUAVAWHA_AA]A\_]@USVWAT
AVAWHA_AA\_[]t$ UWAVH@USVWAVHUVWAVAWHh
VWATAVAWHUVWAVAWHUVWATAUAVAWHpA_AA]A\_]WATAUAVAWH0A_AA]A\_L$
UVWATAUAVAWH@A_AA]A\_]UVWATAUAVAWH`A_AA]A\_]UVWATAUAVAWHpA_AA]A\_]@USVWATAV
AWHD$0fD9 tA_AA\_[]"
```

Due to the size of the example project, we will be diving into the code for each of the different components before running the applications at the end of this section, in the following order:

- The .NET Core library for common code between the two applications
- The ASP.NET Blazor web application for running the prediction
- The .NET Core console application for feature extraction and training

Diving into the library

The classes and enumerations that were changed or added are as follows:

- FileClassificationResponseItem
- Converters
- ExtensionMethods
- HashingExtension
- FileData
- FileDataPrediction
- FileClassificationFeatureExtractor
- FileClassificationPredictor
- FileClassificationTrainer

The Constants and BaseML classes remain unmodified from Chapter 8, *Using ML.NET with .NET Core and Forecasting*.

> Due to the nature of this application and that of production applications, where there are multiple platforms and/or ways to execute shared code, a library is used in this chapter's example application. The benefit of using a library is that all common code can reside in a portable and dependency-free manner. Expanding the functionality in this sample application to include desktop or mobile applications would be a much easier lift than having the code either duplicated or kept in the actual applications.

The FileClassificationResponseItem class

The FileClassificationResponseItem class is the common class that contains the properties that are used to feed our model, and is also used to return back to the end user in the web application.

1. First, we define the TRUE and FALSE mapping to 1.0f and 0.0f respectively, like this:

```
private const float TRUE = 1.0f;
private const float FALSE = 0.0f;
```

2. Next, we add all of the properties to be used to feed our model and display it back to the end user in the web application. The `FileSize`, `Is64Bit`, `NumImports`, `NumImportFunctions`, `NumExportFunctions`, `IsSigned`, and `Strings` properties are used specifically as features in our model. The `SHA1Sum`, `Confidence`, `IsMalicious`, and `ErrorMessage` properties are used to return our classification back to the end user, as illustrated in the following code block:

```
public string SHA1Sum { get; set; }

public double Confidence { get; set; }

public bool IsMalicious { get; set; }

public float FileSize { get; set; }

public float Is64Bit { get; set; }

public float NumImports { get; set; }

public float NumImportFunctions { get; set; }

public float NumExportFunctions { get; set; }

public float IsSigned { get; set; }

public string Strings { get; set; }

public string ErrorMessage { get; set; }
```

3. Next, we have the constructor method. The constructor, as you can see, has a byte array as a parameter. This was done to facilitate both the training and prediction paths in both of the applications, the idea being that the raw file bytes will come into the constructor from a `File.ReadAllBytes` call or other mechanisms, to provide flexibility. From there, we use the `PeNet` NuGet package. This package provides an easy-to-use interface for extracting features from a Windows Executable (also known as a PE file). For the scope of this application, a couple of features were chosen to be extracted and stored into the respective properties, as shown in the following code block:

```
public FileClassificationResponseItem(byte[] fileBytes)
{
    SHA1Sum = fileBytes.ToSHA1();
    Confidence = 0.0;
    IsMalicious = false;
```

```
        FileSize = fileBytes.Length;

        try
        {
            var peFile = new PeNet.PeFile(fileBytes);

            Is64Bit = peFile.Is64Bit ? TRUE : FALSE;

            try
            {
                NumImports = peFile.ImageImportDescriptors.Length;
            }
            catch
            {
                NumImports = 0.0f;
            }

            NumImportFunctions = peFile.ImportedFunctions.Length;

            if (peFile.ExportedFunctions != null)
            {
                NumExportFunctions = peFile.ExportedFunctions.Length;
            }

            IsSigned = peFile.IsSigned ? TRUE : FALSE;

            Strings = fileBytes.ToStringsExtraction();
        }
        catch (Exception)
        {
            ErrorMessage = $"Invalid file ({SHA1Sum}) -
                                only PE files are supported";
        }
    }
```

The FileData class

The FileData class, as with previous containers of prediction data, provides our model
with the fields necessary to provide a file classification. In addition, we overrode
the ToString method to ease the exporting of this data to a **comma-separated values
(CSV)** file during our feature extraction step, as follows:

```
public class FileData
{
    [LoadColumn(0)]
    public float FileSize { get; set; }
```

```
    [LoadColumn(1)]
    public float Is64Bit { get; set; }

    [LoadColumn(2)]
    public float NumberImportFunctions { get; set; }

    [LoadColumn(3)]
    public float NumberExportFunctions { get; set; }

    [LoadColumn(4)]
    public float IsSigned { get; set; }

    [LoadColumn(5)]
    public float NumberImports { get; set; }

    [LoadColumn(6)]
    public bool Label { get; set; }

    [LoadColumn(7)]
    public string Strings { get; set; }

    public override string ToString() =>
            $"{FileSize}\t{Is64Bit}\t{NumberImportFunctions}\t" +
            $"{NumberExportFunctions}\t{IsSigned}\t{NumberImports}\t" +
            $"{Label}\t\"{Strings}\"";
}
```

The FileDataPrediction class

The `FileDataPrediction` class contains the prediction's classification and probability properties to return to the end user in our web application, as shown in the following code block:

```
public class FileDataPrediction
{
    public bool Label { get; set; }

    public bool PredictedLabel { get; set; }

    public float Score { get; set; }

    public float Probability { get; set; }
}
```

The Converters class

The `Converters` class provides an extension method to convert the `FileClassificationResponseItem` class—reviewed earlier in this section—to the `FileData` class. By making an extension method, as shown in the following code block, we can quickly and cleanly convert between the application container and our model-only container:

```
public static class Converters
{
    public static FileData ToFileData(
                    this FileClassificationResponseItem fileClassification)
    {
        return new FileData
        {
            Is64Bit = fileClassification.Is64Bit,
            IsSigned = fileClassification.IsSigned,
            NumberImports = fileClassification.NumImports,
            NumberImportFunctions = fileClassification.NumImportFunctions,
            NumberExportFunctions = fileClassification.NumExportFunctions,
            FileSize = fileClassification.FileSize,
            Strings = fileClassification.Strings
        };
    }
}
```

The ExtensionMethods class

The `ExtensionMethods` class, as shown in previous chapters, contains helper extension methods. In this example, we will be adding in the `ToStrings` extension method. Strings are a highly popular first pass and an easy-to-capture feature when making a classification of a file. Let's dive into the method, as follows:

1. First, we define two new constants for handling the buffer size and the encoding. As mentioned earlier, `1252` is the encoding in which Windows Executables are encoded, as shown in the following code block:

```
private const int BUFFER_SIZE = 2048;
private const int FILE_ENCODING = 1252;
```

2. The next change is the addition of the `ToStringsExtraction` method itself and defining our regular expression, as follows:

```
public static string ToStringsExtraction(this byte[] data)
{
    var stringRex = new Regex(@"[ -~\t]{8,}",
                              RegexOptions.Compiled);
```

This regular expression is what we will use to traverse the file's bytes.

3. Next, we initialize the `StringBuilder` class and check if the passed-in byte array is null or empty (if it is, we can't process it), like this:

```
var stringLines = new StringBuilder();

if (data == null || data.Length == 0)
{
    return stringLines.ToString();
}
```

4. Now that we have confirmed there are bytes in the passed-in array, we only want to take up to 65536 bytes. The reason for this is that if the file is 100 MB, this operation could take significant time to perform. Feel free to adjust this number and see the efficacy results. The code is shown here:

```
var dataToProcess = data.Length > 65536 ?
data.Take(65536).ToArray() : data;
```

5. Now that we have the bytes we are going to analyze, we will loop through and extract lines of text found in the bytes, as follows:

```
using (var ms = new MemoryStream(dataToProcess, false))
{
    using (var streamReader = new StreamReader(ms,
                      Encoding.GetEncoding(FILE_ENCODING),
                      false, BUFFER_SIZE, false))
    {
        while (!streamReader.EndOfStream)
        {
            var line = streamReader.ReadLine();

            if (string.IsNullOrEmpty(line))
            {
                continue;
            }

            line = line.Replace("^", "").Replace(")",
```

```
                                    "").Replace("-", "");

            stringLines.Append(string.Join(string.Empty,
                stringRex.Matches(line).Where(a =>
                    !string.IsNullOrEmpty(a.Value) &&
                    !string.IsNullOrWhiteSpace(a.Value)).ToList()));
        }
    }
}
```

6. Finally, we simply return the lines joined into a single string, like this:

```
return string.Join(string.Empty, stringLines);
```

The HashingExtensions class

The new `HashingExtensions` class converts our byte array to a SHA1 string. The reason for not putting this with our other extension methods is to provide a common class to potentially hold SHA256, ssdeep, or other hashes (especially given the recent SHA1 collisions, proving SHA1 to be insecure).

For this method, we're using the built-in .NET Core `SHA1` class, and then converting it to a Base64 string with a call to `ToBase64String`, as follows:

```
public static class HashingExtension
{
    public static string ToSHA1(this byte[] data)
    {
        var sha1 = System.Security.Cryptography.SHA1.Create();

        var hash = sha1.ComputeHash(data);

        return Convert.ToBase64String(hash);
    }
}
```

The FileClassificationFeatureExtractor class

The `FileClassificationFeatureExtractor` class contains our `Extract` and `ExtractFolder` methods:

1. First, our `ExtractFolder` method takes in the folder path and the output file that will contain our feature extraction, as shown in the following code block:

```
private void ExtractFolder(string folderPath, string outputFile)
{
    if (!Directory.Exists(folderPath))
    {
        Console.WriteLine($"{folderPath} does not exist");

        return;
    }

    var files = Directory.GetFiles(folderPath);

    using (var streamWriter =
        new StreamWriter(Path.Combine(AppContext.BaseDirectory,
                        $"../../../../{outputFile}")))
    {
        foreach (var file in files)
        {
            var extractedData = new
                    FileClassificationResponseItem(
                        File.ReadAllBytes(file)).ToFileData();

            extractedData.Label = !file.Contains("clean");

            streamWriter.WriteLine(extractedData.ToString());
        }
    }

    Console.WriteLine($"Extracted {files.Length} to {outputFile}");
}
```

2. Next, we use the `Extract` method to call both the training and test extraction, as follows:

```
public void Extract(string trainingPath, string testPath)
{
    ExtractFolder(trainingPath, Constants.SAMPLE_DATA);
    ExtractFolder(testPath, Constants.TEST_DATA);
}
```

The FileClassificationPredictor class

The `FileClassificationPredictor` class provides the interface for both our command-line and web applications, using an overloaded `Predict` method:

1. The first `Predict` method is for our command-line application that simply takes in the filename and is called into the overload in *Step 2* after loading in the bytes, as follows:

```
public FileClassificationResponseItem Predict(string fileName)
{
    var bytes = File.ReadAllBytes(fileName);

    return Predict(new FileClassificationResponseItem(bytes));
}
```

2. The second implementation is for our web application that takes the `FileClassificationResponseItem` object, creates our prediction engine, and returns the prediction data, as follows:

```
public FileClassificationResponseItem
Predict(FileClassificationResponseItem file)
{
    if (!File.Exists(Common.Constants.MODEL_PATH))
    {
        file.ErrorMessage = $"Model not found (
                            {Common.Constants.MODEL_PATH}) -
                            please train the model first";

        return file;
    }

    ITransformer mlModel;

    using (var stream = new FileStream(Common.Constants.MODEL_PATH,
                FileMode.Open, FileAccess.Read, FileShare.Read))
    {
        mlModel = MlContext.Model.Load(stream, out _);
    }

    var predictionEngine =
                MlContext.Model.CreatePredictionEngine<FileData,
                FileDataPrediction>(mlModel);

    var prediction = predictionEngine.Predict(file.ToFileData());

    file.Confidence = prediction.Probability;
```

```
file.IsMalicious = prediction.PredictedLabel;

return file;
}
```

The FileClassificationTrainer class

The last class added in the library is the `FileClassificationTrainer` class. This class supports the use of the `FastTree` ML.NET trainer, as well as utilizing our features we have extracted from the files:

1. The first change is the use of the `FileData` class to read the CSV file into the `dataView` property, as shown in the following code block:

```
var dataView =
MlContext.Data.LoadFromTextFile<FileData>(trainingFileName,
hasHeader: false);
```

2. Next, we map our `FileData` features to create our pipeline, as follows:

```
var dataProcessPipeline =
    MlContext.Transforms.NormalizeMeanVariance(
                        nameof(FileData.FileSize))
    .Append(MlContext.Transforms.NormalizeMeanVariance(
            nameof(FileData.Is64Bit)))
    .Append(MlContext.Transforms.NormalizeMeanVariance(
            nameof(FileData.IsSigned)))
    .Append(MlContext.Transforms.NormalizeMeanVariance(
            nameof(FileData.NumberImportFunctions)))
    .Append(MlContext.Transforms.NormalizeMeanVariance(
            nameof(FileData.NumberExportFunctions)))
    .Append(MlContext.Transforms.NormalizeMeanVariance(
            nameof(FileData.NumberImports)))
    .Append(MlContext.Transforms.Text.FeaturizeText(
            "FeaturizeText", nameof(FileData.Strings)))
    .Append(MlContext.Transforms.Concatenate(FEATURES,
            nameof(FileData.FileSize), nameof(FileData.Is64Bit),
            nameof(FileData.IsSigned),
            nameof(FileData.NumberImportFunctions),
            nameof(FileData.NumberExportFunctions),
            nameof(FileData.NumberImports), "FeaturizeText"));
```

3. Lastly, we initialize our `FastTree` algorithm, as follows:

```
var trainer = MlContext.BinaryClassification.Trainers.FastTree(
                    labelColumnName: nameof(FileData.Label),
```

```
featureColumnName: FEATURES,
numberOfLeaves: 2,
numberOfTrees: 1000,
minimumExampleCountPerLeaf: 1,
learningRate: 0.2);
```

The rest of the method is similar to our previous binary classification `Train` method in `Chapter 5`, *Clustering Models*.

Diving into the web application

With the library code having been reviewed, the next component is the web application. As discussed in the opening section, our web application is an ASP.NET Core Blazor application. For the scope of this example, we are using standard approaches for handling the backend and frontend. The architecture of this app combines both Blazor and ASP.NET Core—specifically, using ASP.NET Core to handle the REST service component of the app.

The files we will be diving into in this section are the following ones:

- `UploadController`
- `Startup`
- `Index.razor`

The UploadController class

The purpose of the `UploadController` class is to handle the server-side processing of the file once submitted. For those having used ASP.NET MVC or Web API in the past, this controller should look very familiar:

1. The first thing to note is the attribute tags decorating the class. The `ApiController` attribute configures the controller to handle HTTP APIs, while the `Route` tag indicates the controller will be listening on the `/Upload` path, as shown in the following code block:

```
[ApiController]
[Route("[controller]")]
public class UploadController : ControllerBase
```

2. The next thing to note is the use of **Dependency Injection (DI)** in the constructor of `UploadController` passing in the predictor object. DI is a powerful approach to providing access to singleton objects such as `FileClassificationPredictor` or databases, and is illustrated in the following code block:

```
private readonly FileClassificationPredictor _predictor;

public UploadController(FileClassificationPredictor predictor)
{
    _predictor = predictor;
}
```

3. Next, we create a helper method to handle taking the `IFormFile` from the HTTP post and returning all of the bytes, as follows:

```
private static byte[] GetBytesFromPost(IFormFile file)
{
    using (var ms = new BinaryReader(file.OpenReadStream()))
    {
        return ms.ReadBytes((int)file.Length);
    }
}
```

4. Lastly, we create the `Post` method. The `HttpPost` attribute tells the routing engine to listen for only a `HttpPost` call. The method handles taking the output of the `GetBytesFromPost` method call, creates the `FileClassificationResponseItem` object, and then returns the prediction, as shown in the following code block:

```
[HttpPost]
public FileClassificationResponseItem Post(IFormFile file)
{
    if (file == null)
    {
        return null;
    }

    var fileBytes = GetBytesFromPost(file);

    var responseItem = new FileClassificationResponseItem(
                                                fileBytes);

    return _predictor.Predict(responseItem);
}
```

The Startup class

The Startup class in both an ASP.NET Core and Blazor app controls the initialization of the various services used in the web application. Two major changes have been made to the Startup template that comes with Visual Studio, as follows:

1. The first change is in the ConfigureServices method. Because this was a combined application of both ASP.NET Core and Blazor, we need to call the AddControllers method. In addition, we are going to utilize DI and initialize the predictor object once, prior to adding it as a singleton, as shown in the following code block:

```
public void ConfigureServices(IServiceCollection services)
{
    services.AddRazorPages();
    services.AddControllers();
    services.AddServerSideBlazor();

    services.AddSingleton<FileClassificationPredictor>();
    services.AddSingleton<HttpClient>();
}
```

2. The second change comes in the Configure method. The first thing is to register the CodePages instance. Without this call, the feature extraction call to reference the Windows-1252 encoding will cause an exception (we will add this call to the trainer application as well, in the next section). The second thing is to configure the use of MapControllerRoute, as illustrated in the following code block:

```
public void Configure(IApplicationBuilder app, IWebHostEnvironment env)
{
    Encoding.RegisterProvider(CodePagesEncodingProvider.Instance);

    if (env.IsDevelopment())
    {
        app.UseDeveloperExceptionPage();
    }
    else
    {
        app.UseExceptionHandler("/Error");
    }

    app.UseStaticFiles();

    app.UseRouting();
```

```
app.UseEndpoints(endpoints =>
{
    endpoints.MapControllerRoute("default",
            "{controller=Home}/{action=Index}/{id?}");
    endpoints.MapBlazorHub();
    endpoints.MapFallbackToPage("/_Host");
});
}
```

The Index.razor file

The Index.razor file contains the frontend to our file classification web application. In addition, it contains the REST call to our UploadController class described earlier in this section. For this deep dive, we will specifically look at the Blazor code block, as follows:

1. The first thing to note is the declaration of our FileClassificationResponseItem class. We define the variable in this block, as it will allow access throughout the page. The second element is the declaration of our HandleSelection method, as illustrated in the following code block:

```
FileClassificationResponseItem _classificationResponseItem;

async Task HandleSelection(IEnumerable<IFileListEntry> files) {
```

2. Next, we take the first file, convert it to an array of bytes, and create the MultipartFormdataContent object to POST to the previously described Post method, as follows:

```
var file = files.FirstOrDefault();

if (file != null)
{
    var ms = new MemoryStream();
    await file.Data.CopyToAsync(ms);

    var content = new MultipartFormDataContent {
        {
            new ByteArrayContent(ms.GetBuffer()), "file", file.Name
        }
    };
```

3. Lastly, we POST the file to our `UploadController` endpoint and asynchronously await the response from our ML.NET prediction, before assigning the response to our response variable, `_classificationResponseItem`, as follows:

```
var response = await
client.PostAsync("http://localhost:5000/upload/", content);

var jsonResponse = await response.Content.ReadAsStringAsync();

_classificationResponseItem =
JsonSerializer.Deserialize<FileClassificationResponseItem>(jsonResp
onse, new JsonSerializerOptions
{
    PropertyNameCaseInsensitive = true
});
```

Diving into the trainer application

Now that we have reviewed the shared library and the web application, let's dive into the trainer application.

We will review the following files:

- `ProgramArguments`
- `ProgramActions`
- `Program`

The ProgramArguments class

Building off the work in the `ProgramArguments` class detailed in Chapter 8, *Using ML.NET with .NET Core and Forecasting*, we are only making one addition to the class. This change adds properties to store the `Testing` and `Training` folder paths, and is illustrated in the following code block:

```
public string TestingFolderPath { get; set; }

public string TrainingFolderPath { get; set; }
```

Unlike the previous chapter, feature extraction is based on a number of Windows executable files, as opposed to just an included CSV file.

The ProgramActions enumeration

The first change is in the `ProgramActions` enumeration. In Chapter 8, *Using ML.NET with .NET Core and Forecasting*, we had only training and prediction. However, as mentioned earlier in this chapter, we now also have `FeatureExtraction` to perform. To add support, we simply add `FEATURE_EXTRACTOR` to the enumeration, like so:

```
public enum ProgramActions
{
    FEATURE_EXTRACTOR,
    TRAINING,
    PREDICT
}
```

The Program class

Inside the `Program` class, there are only two changes from the previous chapter's overhaul of the command-line argument parsing, as follows:

1. First, we need to register the `CodePages` encoder instance to properly read the Windows-1252 encoding from the files as we did in the web application, as follows:

   ```
   Encoding.RegisterProvider(CodePagesEncodingProvider.Instance);
   ```

2. We then can use a simplified and strongly typed switch case to handle our three actions, as follows:

   ```
   switch (arguments.Action)
   {
       case ProgramActions.FEATURE_EXTRACTOR:
           new FileClassificationFeatureExtractor().Extract(
                   arguments.TrainingFolderPath,
                   arguments.TestingFolderPath);
           break;
       case ProgramActions.PREDICT:
           var prediction = new
                       FileClassificationPredictor().Predict(
                   arguments.PredictionFileName);

           Console.WriteLine(
                   $"File is {(prediction.IsMalicious ? "malicious" :
                       "clean")} with a {prediction.Confidence:P2}%
                       confidence");
           break;
   ```

```
case ProgramActions.TRAINING:
    new FileClassificationTrainer().Train(
                        arguments.TrainingFileName,
                        arguments.TestingFileName);
    break;
default:
    Console.WriteLine($"Unhandled action {arguments.Action}");
    break;
}
```

Running the trainer application

To begin, we will need to first run the `chapter09.trainer` application to perform feature extraction and training of our model. To run the trainer application, the process is nearly identical to the sample application shown in Chapter 3, *Regression Model*, with the addition of passing in the test dataset folder path when training, and we will follow these steps:

1. We will run the trainer application, passing in the paths to the training and test folders to perform feature extraction, as follows:

   PS chapter09\chapter09.trainer\bin\Debug\netcoreapp3.1>
   .\chapter09.trainer.exe trainingfolderpath
   ..\..\..\..\TrainingData\ testingfolderpath ..\..\..\..\TestData
   Extracted 14 to sampledata.data
   Extracted 14 to testdata.data

   Included in the code repository are two pre-feature extracted files (`sampledata.csv` and `testdata.csv`) to allow you to train a model without performing your own feature extraction. If you would like to perform your own feature extraction, create a `TestData` and `TrainingData` folder. Populate these folders with a sampling of **PowerShell (PS1)**, **Windows Executables (EXE)** and **Microsoft Word documents (DOCX)**.

2. Now, we will again run the application to train the model based on *Step 1* sample and test data exports. The resulting model (`fileclassification.mdl`) will be in the same folder as the executable, as follows:

   PS chapter09\chapter09.trainer\bin\Debug\netcoreapp3.1>
   .\chapter09.trainer.exe action training trainingfilename
   ..\..\..\..\sampledata.data testingfilename
   ..\..\..\..\testdata.data
   Entropy: 0.5916727785823275

```
Log Loss: 12.436063032030377
Log Loss Reduction: -20.018480961432264
```

Feel free to modify the values and see how the prediction changes based on the dataset on which the model was trained. A few areas of experimentation from this point might be to do the following:

- Tweak the hyperparameters reviewed in the `Trainer` class—such as the `numberOfLeaves`, `numberOfTrees`, and `learningRate`—to see how accuracy is affected.
- Add new features to the `FileData` class, such as specific imports, instead of using just the count.
- Add more variation to the training and sample set to get a better sampling of data.

For convenience, the GitHub repository includes both the `testdata.csv` and `sampledata.csv` files.

Running the web application

Now that our model has been trained, we can run our web application and test the submission of a file. You must first build the web application if you haven't already. This will create the `bin\debug\netcoreapp3.1` folder. After building the web application, copy the model we trained in the previous section. At this point, start the web application. Upon starting, you should see the following in your default browser:

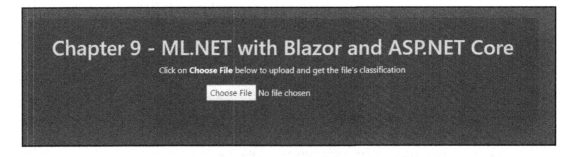

Proceed to click on the **Choose File** button, select an `.exe` or `.dll` file, and you should see the following results from our model:

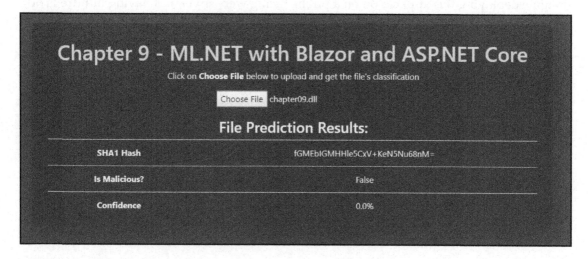

Feel free to try various files on your machine to see the confidence score, and if you receive a false positive, perhaps add additional features to the model to correct the classification.

Exploring additional ideas for improvements

Now that we have completed our deep dive, there are a couple of additional elements to possibly further enhance the application. A few ideas are discussed next.

Logging

As with our previous chapter's deep dive into logging, adding logging could be crucial to remotely understand when an error occurs on a web application. Logging utilizing NLog (`https://nlog-project.org/`) or a similar open source project is highly recommended as your application complexity increases. This will allow you to log to a file, console, or third-party logging solution—such as Loggly—at varying levels.

Utilizing a caching layer

Imagine deploying this application on a public-facing web server and having hundreds of concurrent users. Chances are that users might upload the same file—caching the results in memory would avoid unnecessary CPU processing to run the prediction every time. Some caching options include utilizing the ASP.NET in-memory caching, or external caching databases such as Redis. These are both available via NuGet packages.

Utilizing a database

On a similar note to the caching suggestion, recording the results in a database could avoid unnecessary CPU processing. A logical choice would be to utilize a NoSQL database such as MongoDB. Using the SHA1 hash as the key and the value as the full JSON response could significantly improve performance in a high-traffic scenario. MongoDB has a .NET interface available on NuGet called `MongoDB.Driver`. Version 2.10.0 is the latest at the time of writing.

Summary

Over the course of this chapter, we have discussed what goes into a production-ready ASP.NET Core Blazor web application architecture, using the work performed in previous chapters as a foundation. We also created a brand new file classification web application utilizing the FastTree binary classifier from ML.NET. Lastly, we also discussed some ways to further enhance an ASP.NET Core application (and production applications in general).

In the next chapter, we will deep dive into creating a production web browser using the content of a web page to determine if the content is malicious or not, using ML.NET's sentiment analysis and the UWP framework.

Using ML.NET with UWP

10

Now that we have established how to create a production-grade .NET Core console application, in this chapter, we will deep dive into creating a fully functional Windows 10 application with the **Universal Windows Platform** (**UWP**) framework. This application will utilize an ML.NET binary classification model to make web-page-content classifications, in order to determine if the content is benign or malicious. In addition, we will explore breaking your code into a component-based architecture, using a .NET Standard Library to share between our desktop application and the console application that will train our model. By the end of the chapter, you should have a firm grasp of designing and coding a production-grade UWP desktop application with ML.NET.

The following topics will be covered in this chapter:

- Breaking down the UWP application
- Creating the web browser classification application
- Exploring additional production-application enhancements

Breaking down the UWP architecture

At a high level, UWP provides an easy framework to create rich desktop applications for Windows 10. As discussed, with .NET Core, UWP allows the targeting of x86, x64, and **Advanced RISC Machine** (**ARM**). At the time of this writing, ARM is not supported with ML.NET. In addition, UWP applications can also be written with JavaScript and HTML.

A typical UWP desktop application includes the following core code elements:

- Views
- Models
- View Models

These components form a common app architecture principle of the **Model-View-ViewModel**, otherwise known as **MVVM**. In addition to the code components, images and audio are also common, depending on the nature of your application or game.

Similarly to mobile apps on the Android and iOS platforms, each app is sandboxed to specific permissions that you, the developer, request upon installation. Therefore, as you develop your own UWP applications, request only the required access that your app absolutely requires.

For the example application we will be creating in this chapter, we only require access to the internet as a client, as found in the **Capabilities** tab labeled **Internet (Client)**, as shown in the following screenshot:

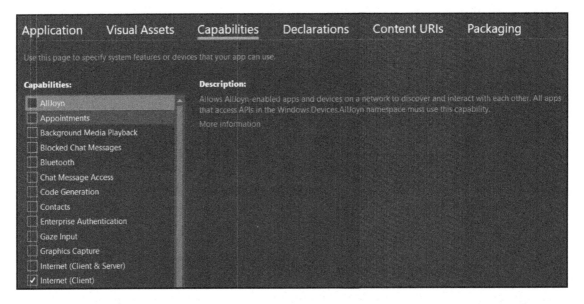

The **Internet (Client)** and other permissions are defined in the `Package.appxmanifest` file found in the root of UWP applications, under the **Capabilities** tab. This file is shown in the Visual Studio Solution Explorer screenshot in the later *Exploring the project architecture* section.

To prepare for our deep dive into integrating ML.NET in a UWP application, let's dive into the three core components found in a UWP application.

Views

Views, as we defined in the previous chapter's Blazor discussion, contain the **user interface (UI)** components of an application. Views in UWP development, such as those found in **Windows Presentation Foundation (WPF)** and Xamarin.Forms, use the **Extensible Application Markup Language (XAML)** syntax. Those familiar with modern web development with Bootstrap's Grid pattern will be able to quickly see the parallels as we deep dive into this later in this chapter.

The biggest differentiation between web development and UWP development is the powerful two-way binding XAML views when used with the MVVM principle. As you will see in the deep dive, XAML binding eliminates the manual setting and getting of values in code behinds, as you might have performed in Windows Forms or WebForms projects previously.

For applications using the web approach, HTML would define your View as with our Blazor project in Chapter 9, *Using ML.NET with ASP.NET Core.*

Models

Models provide the container of data between the View and View Model. Think of the Model as purely the transport for containing the data between the View and View Model. For example, if you had a movie list, a List collection of MovieItems would be defined in your MovieListingModel class. This container class would be instantiated and populated in the View Model, to be in turn bound in your View.

View Models

View Models provide the business-logic layer for populating your Model, and thereby your View indirectly. As mentioned previously, the MVVM binding provided in UWP development eases the management of trigger points to ensure your UI layer is up to date. This is achieved through the use of implementing the INotifyPropertyChanged interface in our View Model. For each property that we want to bind to our UI, we simply call OnPropertyChanged. The power behind this is that you can have complex forms with triggers within the setter of other properties, without having conditionals and endless code to handle the complexities.

If you want to deep dive further into UWP development, Channel9 from Microsoft has a series called *Windows 10 Development for Absolute Beginners* that covers all of the main aspects of UWP development: `https://channel9.msdn.com/Series/Windows-10-development-for-absolute-beginners`.

Creating the web browser classification application

As mentioned earlier, the application we will be creating is a web browser classification application. Using the knowledge garnered in the logistic classification chapter, we will be using the `SdcaLogisticRegression` algorithm to take the text content of a web page, featurize the text, and provide a confidence level of maliciousness. In addition, we will be integrating this technique into a Windows 10 UWP application that mimics a web browser—effectively on navigation to a page—running the model, and making a determination as to whether the page was malicious. If found to be malicious, we redirect to a warning page. While in a real-world scenario this might prove too slow to run on every page, the benefits of a highly secured web browser, depending on the environment requirements might far outweigh the slight overhead running our model incurs.

As with previous chapters, the completed project code, sample dataset, and project files can be downloaded from `https://github.com/PacktPublishing/Hands-On-Machine-Learning-With-ML.NET/tree/master/chapter10`.

Exploring the project architecture

With this chapter, we will dive into a native Windows 10 desktop application. As mentioned in the first section of this chapter, we will be using the UWP framework to create our application.

No additional ML.NET NuGet packages are needed for this sample application. However, we will be using the `HtmlAgilityPack` NuGet package to provide a quick method to extract the text from a given web page. At the time of this writing, version 1.11.18 was the latest version and is the version used in this example.

In the following screenshot, you will find the Visual Studio Solution Explorer view of the solution. Given that this example comprises three separate projects (more akin to a production scenario), the amount of both new and significantly modified files is quite large. We will review in detail each of the new files shown in the solution screenshot, later on in this section:

The `sampledata.csv` file (found in the `Data` folder in the code repository) contains eight rows of extracted text from URLs found in the `trainingURLList.csv` file (also found in the `Data` folder). Feel free to adjust the URL list file to test websites you frequently visit. Here is a snippet of one such row:

```
False|BingImagesVideosMapsNewsShoppingMSNOfficeOutlookWordExcelPowerPointOn
eNoteSwayOneDriveCalendarPeopleSigninRewardsDownloadtoday'simagePlaytoday'sq
uizTheTajMahalinAgraforIndia'sRepublicDay©MicheleFalzone/plainpictureIt'sRe
publicDayinIndiaImageofthedayJan26,2020It'sRepublicDayinIndia©MicheleFalzon
e/plainpictureForIndia's70thRepublicDay
```

In addition to the `sampledata.csv` file, we also added the `testdata.csv` file that contains additional data points to test the newly trained model against and to evaluate. Here is a snippet of a sample row of the data inside of `testdata.csv`:

```
True|USATODAY:LatestWorldandUSNews-
USATODAY.comSUBSCRIBENOWtogethomedeliveryNewsSportsEntertainmentLifeMoneyTe
chTravelOpinionWeatherIconHumidityPrecip.WindsOpensettingsSettingsEnterCity
NameCancelSetClosesettingsFullForecastCrosswordsInvestigationsAppsBest-
SellingBooksCartoons
```

Due to the size of the example project, we will be diving into the code for each of the different components before running the applications at the end of this section in the following order:

- .NET Standard Library for common code between the two applications
- Windows 10 UWP browser application
- .NET Core console application for feature extraction and training

Diving into the library

Due to the nature of this application and that of production applications where there are multiple platforms and/or ways to execute shared code, a library is being used in this chapter's example application. The benefit of using a library is that all common code can reside in a portable and dependency-free manner. Expanding the functionality in this sample application to include other platforms such as Linux or Mac applications with Xamarin would be a much easier lift than having the code either duplicated or kept in the actual applications.

Classes and enumerations that were changed or added in the library are as follows:

- `Constants`
- `WebPageResponseItem`
- `Converters`
- `ExtensionMethods`
- `WebPageInputItem`
- `WebPagePredictionItem`
- `WebContentFeatureExtractor`
- `WebContentPredictor`
- `WebContentTrainer`

The `Classification`, `TrainerActions`, and `BaseML` classes remain unmodified from `Chapter 9`, *Using ML.NET with ASP.NET Core*.

The Constants class

The `Constants` class, as used in all of our examples to this point, is the common class that contains our constant values used in our library, trainer, and UWP applications. For this chapter, the `MODEL_NAME` and `MALICIOUS_THRESHOLD` properties were added to hold our model's name and an arbitrary threshold for when we should decide to classify our prediction as malicious or not, respectively. If you find your model too sensitive, try adjusting this threshold, like this:

```
public static class Constants
{
    public const string MODEL_NAME = "webcontentclassifier.mdl";

    public const string SAMPLE_DATA = "sampledata.csv";

    public const string TEST_DATA = "testdata.csv";

    public const double MALICIOUS_THRESHOLD = .5;
}
```

The WebPageResponseItem class

The WebPageResponseItem class is our container class between our predictor and application. This class contains the properties we set after running the predictor and then use to display in our desktop application, as shown in the following code block:

```
public class WebPageResponseItem
{
    public double Confidence { get; set; }

    public bool IsMalicious { get; set; }

    public string Content { get; set; }

    public string ErrorMessage { get; set; }

    public WebPageResponseItem()
    {
    }

    public WebPageResponseItem(string content)
    {
        Content = content;
    }
}
```

The Converters class

The Converters class has been adjusted to provide an extension method to convert our container class into the type our model expects. In this example, we have the Content property, which simply maps to the HTMLContent variable in the WebPageInputItem class, as follows:

```
public static WebPageInputItem ToWebPageInputItem(this WebPageResponseItem
webPage)
{
    return new WebPageInputItem
    {
        HTMLContent = webPage.Content
    };
}
```

The ExtensionMethods class

The `ExtensionMethods` class, as discussed previously in `Chapter 9`, *Using ML.NET with ASP.NET Core*, has been expanded to include the `ToWebContentString` extension method. In this method, we pass in the URL from which we want to retrieve the web content. Using the previously mentioned `HtmlAgilityPack`, we create an `HtmlWeb` object and call the `Load` method, prior to iterating through the **Document Object Model (DOM)**. Given most websites have extensive scripts and style sheets, our purpose in this example is just to examine the text in the page, thus the filters of script and style nodes in our code. Once the nodes have been traversed and added to a `StringBuilder` object, we return the typecast of that object to a string, as shown in the following code block:

```
public static string ToWebContentString(this string url)
{
    var web = new HtmlWeb();

    var htmlDoc = web.Load(url);
    var sb = new StringBuilder();

    htmlDoc.DocumentNode.Descendants().Where(n => n.Name == "script" ||
                n.Name == "style").ToList().ForEach(n => n.Remove());

    foreach (var node in htmlDoc.DocumentNode.SelectNodes("//text()
                                        [normalize-space(.) != '']"))
    {
        sb.Append(node.InnerText.Trim().Replace(" ", ""));
    }

    return sb.ToString();
}
```

The WebPageInputItem class

The `WebPageInputItem` class is our input object to our model, containing both the label and extracted content of our web page, as shown in the following code block:

```
public class WebPageInputItem
{
    [LoadColumn(0), ColumnName("Label")]
    public bool Label { get; set; }

    [LoadColumn(1)]
    public string HTMLContent { get; set; }
}
```

The WebPagePredictionItem class

The `WebPagePredictionItem` class is the output object from our model, containing the prediction of whether a web page is malicious or benign, in addition to a probability score that the prediction is accurate and the `Score` value used in the evaluation phase of our model creation, as shown in the following code block:

```
public class WebPagePredictionItem
{
    public bool Prediction { get; set; }

    public float Probability { get; set; }

    public float Score { get; set; }
}
```

The WebContentFeatureExtractor class

The `WebContentFeatureExtractor` class contains our `GetContentFile` and `Extract` methods, which operate as follows:

1. First, our `GetContentFile` method takes the `inputFile` and `outputFile` values (the URL list CSV and feature-extracted CSV respectively). It then reads each URL, grabs the content, then outputs to the `outputFile` string, as follows:

```
private static void GetContentFile(string inputFile, string
outputFile)
{
    var lines = File.ReadAllLines(inputFile);

    var urlContent = new List<string>();

    foreach (var line in lines)
    {
        var url = line.Split(',')[0];
        var label = Convert.ToBoolean(line.Split(',')[1]);

        Console.WriteLine($"Attempting to pull HTML from {line}");

        try
        {
            var content = url.ToWebContentString();

            content = content.Replace('|', '-');
```

```
            urlContent.Add($"{label}|{content}");
        }
        catch (Exception)
        {
            Console.WriteLine(
                    $"Failed to pull HTTP Content from {url}");
        }
    }

    File.WriteAllText(
            Path.Combine(AppContext.BaseDirectory, outputFile),
            string.Join(Environment.NewLine, urlContent));
}
```

2. Next, we use the `Extract` method to call both the training and test extraction, passing in the output filenames for both, like this:

```
public void Extract(string trainingURLList, string testURLList,
string trainingOutputFileName, string testingOutputFileName)
{
    GetContentFile(trainingURLList, trainingOutputFileName);

    GetContentFile(testURLList, testingOutputFileName);
}
```

The WebContentPredictor class

The `WebContentPredictor` class provides the interface for both our command line and desktop applications, using an overloaded `Predict` method, described here:

1. The first `Predict` method is for our command-line application that simply takes in the URL and calls into the overload in *Step 3*, after calling the `ToWebContentString` extension method, like this:

```
public WebPageResponseItem Predict(string url) => Predict(new
WebPageResponseItem(url.ToWebContentString()));
```

2. Then, we create the `Initialize` method, in which we load our model from the embedded resource. If successful, the method returns `true`; otherwise, it returns `false`, as shown in the following code block:

```
public bool Initialize()
{
    var assembly = typeof(WebContentPredictor).GetTypeInfo()
                            .Assembly;
```

```
var resource = assembly.GetManifestResourceStream(
                 $"chapter10.lib.Model.{Constants.MODEL_NAME}");

if (resource == null)
{
    return false;
}

_model = MlContext.Model.Load(resource, out _);

return true;
}
```

3. And finally, we call our `Predict` method that creates our prediction engine. Then, we call the predictor's `Predict` method, and then update the `Confidence` and `IsMalicious` properties, prior to returning the updated `WebPageResponseItem` object, as follows:

```
public WebPageResponseItem Predict(WebPageResponseItem webPage)
{
    var predictionEngine = MlContext.Model.CreatePredictionEngine
            <WebPageInputItem, WebPagePredictionItem>(_model);

    var prediction = predictionEngine.Predict(
                        webPage.ToWebPageInputItem());

    webPage.Confidence = prediction.Probability;
    webPage.IsMalicious = prediction.Prediction;

    return webPage;
}
```

The WebContentTrainer class

The `WebContentTrainer` class contains all of the code to train and evaluate our model. As with previous examples, this functionality is self-contained within one method called `Train`:

1. The first change is the use of the `WebPageInputItem` class to read the CSV into the `dataView` object separated by |, as shown in the following code block:

```
var dataView = MlContext.Data.LoadFromTextFile<WebPageInputItem>(
        trainingFileName, hasHeader: false, separatorChar: '|');
```

2. Next, we map our file data features to create our pipeline. In this example, we simply featurize the `HTMLContent` property and pass it to the `SdcaLogisticRegression` trainer, like this:

```
var dataProcessPipeline = MlContext.Transforms.Text
    .FeaturizeText(FEATURES, nameof(WebPageInputItem.HTMLContent))
.Append(MlContext.BinaryClassification.Trainers.SdcaLogisticRegress
ion(labelColumnName: "Label", featureColumnName: FEATURES));
```

3. Then, we fit the model, and save the model to disk, like this:

```
var trainedModel = dataProcessPipeline.Fit(dataView);

MlContext.Model.Save(trainedModel, dataView.Schema,
Path.Combine(AppContext.BaseDirectory, modelFileName));
```

4. Finally, we load in the testing file, and call the `BinaryClassification` evaluation, like this:

```
var testingDataView =
MlContext.Data.LoadFromTextFile<WebPageInputItem>(testingFileName,
hasHeader: false, separatorChar: '|');

IDataView testDataView = trainedModel.Transform(testingDataView);

var modelMetrics = MlContext.BinaryClassification.Evaluate(
    data: testDataView);

Console.WriteLine($"Entropy: {modelMetrics.Entropy}");
Console.WriteLine($"Log Loss: {modelMetrics.LogLoss}");
Console.WriteLine($"Log Loss Reduction:
{modelMetrics.LogLossReduction}");
```

Diving into the UWP browser application

With the library code having been reviewed, the next component is the desktop application. As discussed in the opening section, our desktop application is a UWP application. For the scope of this example, we are using standard approaches for handling the application architecture, following the MVVM approach discussed in the opening section of this chapter.

The files we will be diving into in this section are as follows:

- MainPageViewModel
- MainPage.xaml
- MainPage.xaml.cs

The rest of the files inside the UWP project, such as the tile images and app class files, are untouched from the default Visual Studio UWP application template.

The MainPageViewModel class

The purpose of the MainPageViewModel class is to contain our business logic and control the View:

1. The first thing we do is instantiate our previously discussed WebContentPredictor class to be used to run predictions, as follows:

```
private readonly WebContentPredictor _prediction = new
WebContentPredictor();
```

2. The next block of code handles the power of MVVM for our **GO** button, the web service URL field, and the web classification properties. For each of these properties, we call OnPropertyChanged upon a change in values, which triggers the binding of the View to refresh for any field bound to these properties, as shown in the following code block:

```
private bool _enableGoButton;

public bool EnableGoButton
{
    get => _enableGoButton;

    private set
    {
        _enableGoButton = value;
        OnPropertyChanged();
    }
}

private string _webServiceURL;

public string WebServiceURL
{
    get => _webServiceURL;
```

```
        set
        {
            _webServiceURL = value;

            OnPropertyChanged();

            EnableGoButton = !string.IsNullOrEmpty(value);
        }
    }

    private string _webPageClassification;

    public string WebPageClassification
    {
        get => _webPageClassification;

        set
        {
            _webPageClassification = value;
            OnPropertyChanged();
        }
    }
```

3. Next, we define the `Initialize` method, which calls the predictor's `Initialize` method. The method will return false if the model can't be loaded or found, as follows:

```
public bool Initialize() => _prediction.Initialize();
```

4. Then, we take the entered URL the user entered via the `WebServiceURL` property. From that value, we validate that either `http` or `https` is prefixed. If not, `http://` is prefixed to the URL prior to converting it to a URI, like this:

```
public Uri BuildUri()
{
    var webServiceUrl = WebServiceURL;

    if (!webServiceUrl.StartsWith("http://",
                StringComparison.InvariantCultureIgnoreCase) &&
        !webServiceUrl.StartsWith("https://",
                StringComparison.InvariantCultureIgnoreCase))
    {
        webServiceUrl = $"http://{webServiceUrl}";
    }

    return new Uri(webServiceUrl);
}
```

5. Now, onto our `Classify` method that takes the URL entered from the user. This method calls our `Predict` method, builds our status bar text, and, if found to be malicious, builds the HTML response to send back to our `WebView` object, as follows:

```
public (Classification ClassificationResult, string BrowserContent)
Classify(string url)
{
    var result = _prediction.Predict(url);

    WebPageClassification = $"Webpage is considered
                            {result.Confidence:P1} malicious";

    return result.Confidence < Constants.MALICIOUS_THRESHOLD ?
        (Classification.BENIGN, string.Empty) :
        (Classification.MALICIOUS, $"<html><body bgcolor=\"red\">
            <h2 style=\"text-align: center\">Machine Learning has
            found {WebServiceURL} to be a malicious site and was
            blocked automatically</h2></body></html>");
}
```

6. And lastly, we implement the `OnPropertyChanged` event handler and method that are the standard implementations of the `INotifyPropertyChanged` interface, as discussed in the opening section of this chapter and shown in the following code block:

```
public event PropertyChangedEventHandler PropertyChanged;

protected virtual void OnPropertyChanged([CallerMemberName] string
propertyName = null)
{
    PropertyChanged?.Invoke(this,
                    new PropertyChangedEventArgs(propertyName));
}
```

MainPage.xaml

As discussed in the opening section describing UWP development, XAML markup is used to define your UI. For the scope of this application, our UI is relatively simple:

1. The first thing we define is our `Grid`. In XAML, a `Grid` is a container similar to a `div` element in web development. We then define our Rows. Similar to Bootstrap, (but easier to understand, in my opinion) is to pre-define the height of each row. Setting a row to `Auto` will auto-size the height to the content's height, while an asterisk translates to using all remaining height based on the main container's height, as shown in the following code block:

```
<Grid>
  <Grid.RowDefinitions>
    <RowDefinition Height="Auto" />
    <RowDefinition Height="*" />
    <RowDefinition Height="Auto" />
  </Grid.RowDefinitions>
```

2. Similar to the row definitions in *Step 1*, we pre-define columns. `"Auto"` and `"*"` equate to the same principle as they did for the rows, just in regard to width instead of height, as shown in the following code block:

```
<Grid.ColumnDefinitions>
    <ColumnDefinition Width="*" />
    <ColumnDefinition Width="Auto" />
</Grid.ColumnDefinitions>
```

3. We then define our `TextBox` object for the URL entry. Note the `Binding` call in the `Text` value. This binds the textbox's text field to the `WebServiceURL` property in our View Model, as follows:

```
<TextBox Grid.Row="0" Grid.Column="0" KeyUp="TxtBxUrl_KeyUp"
Text="{Binding WebServiceURL, Mode=TwoWay,
UpdateSourceTrigger=PropertyChanged}" />
```

4. Then, we add the button to mimic a browser's **GO** button, which triggers the navigation. Also, note the use of `Binding` to enable or disable the button itself (which is bound based on text being entered into the URL textbox), as shown in the following code block:

```
<Button Grid.Row="0" Grid.Column="1" Content="GO"
Click="BtnGo_Click" IsEnabled="{Binding EnableGoButton}" />
```

5. We then add the `WebView` control that comes with UWP, as follows:

```
<WebView Grid.Row="1" Grid.Column="0" Grid.ColumnSpan="2"
x:Name="wvMain" NavigationStarting="WvMain_OnNavigationStarting" />
```

6. Lastly, we add our status bar grid and `TextBlock` control to show the classification along the bottom of the window, as follows:

```
<Grid Grid.Column="0" Grid.ColumnSpan="2" Grid.Row="2"
Background="#1e1e1e" Height="30">
    <TextBlock Text="{Binding WebPageClassification, Mode=OneWay}"
Foreground="White" Margin="10,0,0,0" />
</Grid>
```

MainPage.xaml.cs

The `MainPage.xaml.cs` file contains the code behind the XAML view discussed previously:

1. The first thing we define is a wrapper property around the `DataContext` property built into the base `Page` class, as follows:

```
private MainPageViewModel ViewModel => (MainPageViewModel)
DataContext;
```

2. Next, we define the constructor for `MainPage` to initialize the `DataContext` to our `MainPageViewModel` object, as follows:

```
public MainPage()
{
    InitializeComponent();

    DataContext = new MainPageViewModel();
}
```

3. We then override the base `OnNavigatedTo` method to initialize our View Model, and validate the model was loaded properly, as follows:

```
protected override async void OnNavigatedTo(NavigationEventArgs e)
{
    var initialization = ViewModel.Initialize();

    if (initialization)
    {
        return;
    }
```

```
await ShowMessage("Failed to initialize model - verify the
                   model has been created");

Application.Current.Exit();

base.OnNavigatedTo(e);
}
```

4. Next, we add our `ShowMessage` wrapper to provide an easy one-liner to call throughout our application, like this:

```
public async Task<IUICommand> ShowMessage(string message)
{
    var dialog = new MessageDialog(message);

    return await dialog.ShowAsync();
}
```

5. Then, we handle the **GO** button click by calling the `Navigate` method, as follows:

```
private void BtnGo_Click(object sender, RoutedEventArgs e) =>
Navigate();
```

6. We then create our `Navigate` wrapper method, which builds the URI and passes it to the `WebView` object, as follows:

```
private void Navigate()
{
    wvMain.Navigate(ViewModel.BuildUri());
}
```

7. We also want to handle the keyboard input to listen for the user hitting the *Enter* key after entering a URL, to provide the user with the ability to either hit *Enter* or click the **GO** button, like this:

```
private void TxtBxUrl_KeyUp(object sender, KeyRoutedEventArgs e)
{
    if (e.Key == VirtualKey.Enter && ViewModel.EnableGoButton)
    {
        Navigate();
    }
}
```

8. Lastly, we block navigation until a classification can be obtained by hooking into the WebView's `OnNavigationStarting` event, as follows:

```
private void WvMain_OnNavigationStarting(WebView sender,
WebViewNavigationStartingEventArgs args)
{
    if (args.Uri == null)
    {
        return;
    }

    var (classificationResult, browserContent) =
                    ViewModel.Classify(args.Uri.ToString());

    switch (classificationResult)
    {
        case Classification.BENIGN:
            return;
        case Classification.MALICIOUS:
            sender.NavigateToString(browserContent);
            break;
    }
}
```

Diving into the trainer application

Now that we have reviewed the shared library and the desktop application, let us dive into the trainer application. With the major architectural changes being performed in Chapter 8's example, by design the trainer application has only minimal changes to handle the specific class objects used in this chapter's example.

We will review the following files:

- `ProgramArguments`
- `Program`

The ProgramArguments class

Building off the work in Chapter 9's `ProgramArguments` class, we are only making three additions to the class. The first two additions are to include both the `Training` and `Testing` output filenames to provide better flexibility with our example's infrastructure. In addition, the `URL` property holds the URL you can pass, using the command line, into the trainer application to get a prediction, as shown in the following code block:

```
public string TrainingOutputFileName { get; set; }

public string TestingOutputFileName { get; set; }

public string URL { get; set; }
```

The Program class

Inside the `Program` class, we will now modify the `switch case` statement to use the classes/methods from `Chapter 10`, *Using ML.NET with UWP*, as follows:

```
switch (arguments.Action)
{
    case ProgramActions.FEATURE_EXTRACTOR:
        new WebContentFeatureExtractor().Extract(
            arguments.TrainingFileName, arguments.TestingFileName,
            arguments.TrainingOutputFileName,
            arguments.TestingOutputFileName);
        break;
    case ProgramActions.PREDICT:
        var predictor = new WebContentPredictor();

        var initialization = predictor.Initialize();

        if (!initialization)
        {
            Console.WriteLine("Failed to initialize the model");

            return;
        }

        var prediction = predictor.Predict(arguments.URL);

        Console.WriteLine(
            $"URL is {(prediction.IsMalicious ? "malicious" : "clean")}
                with a {prediction.Confidence:P2}% confidence");
        break;
    case ProgramActions.TRAINING:
```

```
        new WebContentTrainer().Train(arguments.TrainingFileName,
               arguments.TestingFileName, arguments.ModelFileName);
        break;
    default:
        Console.WriteLine($"Unhandled action {arguments.Action}");
        break;
}
```

Running the trainer application

To begin running the trainer application, we will need to first run
the `chapter10.trainer` application to perform feature extraction prior to the training of
our model. To run the trainer application, the process is nearly identical to Chapter 9's
sample application, with the addition of passing in the test dataset filename path when
training:

1. Run the trainer application, passing in the paths to the training and test URL list
   CSVs to perform feature extraction, as follows:

```
PS chapter10\trainer\bin\Debug\netcoreapp3.0>
.\chapter10.trainer.exe TrainingFileName
..\..\..\..\Data\trainingURLList.csv TestingFileName
..\..\..\..\Data\testingURLList.csv
Attempting to pull HTML from https://www.google.com, false
Attempting to pull HTML from https://www.bing.com, false
Attempting to pull HTML from https://www.microsoft.com, false
Attempting to pull HTML from https://www8.hp.com/us/en/home.html,
false
Attempting to pull HTML from https://dasmalwerk.eu, true
Attempting to pull HTML from http://vxvault.net, true
Attempting to pull HTML from https://www.tmz.com, true
Attempting to pull HTML from http://openmalware.org, true
Failed to pull HTTP Content from http://openmalware.org
Attempting to pull HTML from https://www.dell.com, false
Attempting to pull HTML from https://www.lenovo.com, false
Attempting to pull HTML from https://www.twitter.com, false
Attempting to pull HTML from https://www.reddit.com, false
Attempting to pull HTML from https://www.tmz.com, true
Attempting to pull HTML from https://www.cnn.com, true
Attempting to pull HTML from https://www.usatoday.com, true
```

2. Run the application to train the model, based on *Step 1*'s sample and test data exports, as follows:

```
PS chapter10\trainer\bin\Debug\netcoreapp3.0>
.\chapter10.trainer.exe ModelFileName webcontentclassifier.mdl
Action TRAINING TrainingFileName ..\..\..\..\Data\sampledata.csv
TestingFileName ..\..\..\..\Data\testdata.csv
Entropy: 0.9852281360342516
Log Loss: 0.7992317560011841
Log Loss Reduction: 0.18878508766684401
```

Feel free to modify the values and see how the prediction changes, based on the dataset on which the model was trained. A few areas of experimentation from this point might be to:

- Tweak the hyperparameters reviewed in the `Trainer` class on the **Stochastic Dual Coordinate Ascent (SDCA)** algorithm, such as `MaximumNumberOfIterations`, to see how accuracy is affected.
- Add new features in addition to simply using the HTML content—perhaps the connection type or the number of scripts.
- Add more variation to the training and sample set to get a better sampling of both benign and malicious content.

For convenience, the GitHub repository includes all of the following data files in the `Data` folder:

- The `testdata.csv` and `sampledata.csv` feature-extracted CSV files
- The `testingURLList.csv` and `trainingURLList.csv` URL list CSV files

Running the browser application

Now that our model has been trained, we can run our desktop application and test the efficacy of the model. To run the example, make sure the chapter10_app is the startup app and hit *F5*. Upon launching our browser application, enter www.google.com, as shown in the following screenshot:

Note the status bar below the web page content in the preceding screenshot, indicating the malicious percentage after running the model. Next, type `dasmalwerk.eu` into your browser (this is a website that the default training URL list pre-classified as malicious), and note the forced redirect, as shown in the following screenshot:

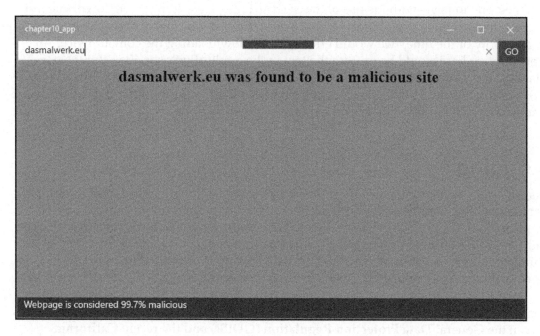

Feel free to try various files on your machine to see the confidence score, and if you receive a false positive, perhaps add additional features to the model to correct the classification.

Additional ideas for improvements

Now that we have completed our deep dive, there are a couple of additional elements to possibly further enhance the application. A few ideas are discussed here.

Single-download optimization

Currently, when a new URL is entered or the page is changed in the `WebView` UWP control, the navigation is halted until a classification can be made. When this occurs—as we detailed previously—with the use of the `HtmlAgilityPack` library, we download and extract the text. If the page is deemed to be clean (as one would more than likely encounter the majority of the time), we would effectively be downloading the content twice. An optimization here would be to store the text in the application's sandbox storage once classification is done, then point the `WebView` object to that stored content. In addition, if this approach is used, add a purge background worker to remove older data so that your end users don't end up with several gigabytes of web page content.

Logging

As with our previous chapter's deep dive into logging, adding logging could be crucial to remotely understand when an error occurs on a desktop application. Unlike our web application in the previous chapter, where your errors would be more than likely server-side and could be accessed remotely, your desktop application could be installed on any number of configurations of Windows 10, with an almost unlimited number of permutations. As mentioned previously, logging utilizing NLog (`https://nlog-project.org/`) or a similar open source project is highly recommended, coupled with a remote logging solution such as Loggly so that you can get error data from your user's machines. Given the **General Data Protection Regulation (GDPR)** and the recent **California Consumer Privacy Act (CCPA)**, ensure that the fact this data is leaving the end user's machines is conveyed, and do not include personal data in these logs.

Utilizing a database

Users typically visit the same websites fairly frequently, therefore storing the classification of a particular website's URL in a local database such as LiteDB (`http://www.litedb.org/`) would significantly improve the performance for the end user. One implementation method would be to store a SHA256 hash of the URL locally as the key, with the classification as the value. Longer term, you could provide a web URL reputation database, with the SHA256 hash of the URL being sent up to a scalable cloud storage solution such as Microsoft's Cosmos DB. Storing the SHA256 hash of the URL avoids any questions from your end users about personally identifiable information and anonymity.

Summary

Over the course of this chapter, we have deep dived into what goes into a production-ready Windows 10 UWP application architecture, using the work performed in previous chapters as a foundation. We also created a brand new web-page-classification Windows 10 application, utilizing the `SdcaLogisticRegression` algorithm from ML.NET. Lastly, we also discussed some ways to further enhance the example application (and production applications in general).

With the conclusion of this chapter, this ends the real-world application section. The next section of the book includes both general machine learning practices in an agile production team and extending ML.NET with TensorFlow and **Open Neural Network Exchange (ONNX)** models. In the next chapter, we will focus on the former.

Section 4: Extending ML.NET

4

This section explains how to use pre-trained models in other formats with ML.NET, including TensorFlow and ONNX. In addition, some of the chapters will cover how to train at scale and the lessons learned using the DMTP project.

This section comprises the following chapters:

- Chapter 11, *Training and Building Production Models*
- Chapter 12, *Using TensorFlow with ML.NET*
- Chapter 13, *Using ONNX with ML.NET*

11
Training and Building Production Models

As we enter the last section of the book, this chapter provides an overview of using machine learning in a production environment. At this point in the book, you have learned the various algorithms that ML.NET provides, and you have created a set of three production applications. With all of this knowledge garnered, your first thought will probably be: how can I immediately create the next killer machine learning app? Prior to jumping right into answering that question, this chapter will help to prepare you for those next steps in that journey. As discussed and utilized in previous chapters, there are three major components of training a model: feature engineering, sample gathering, and creating a training pipeline. In this chapter we will focus on those three components, expanding your thought process for how to succeed in creating a production model, as well as providing some suggested tools for being able to repeat that success with a production-grade training pipeline.

Over the course of this chapter we will discuss the following:

- Investigating feature engineering
- Obtaining training and testing datasets
- Creating your model-building pipeline

Investigating feature engineering

As we have discussed in previous chapters, features are one of the most important components—and objectively the most important component—in the model building process. When approaching a new problem, the main question that arises is: how are you going to solve this problem? For example, a common exploit in the cyber-security world is the use of steganography. Steganography, which dates back to 440 BCE is the practice of hiding data within a container. This container has ranged from drawings, crosswords, music, and pictures, to name a few. In the cyber-security world, steganography is used to hide malicious payloads in files that would otherwise be ignored, such as images, and audio and video files.

Take the following image of a basket of food. This image—created using an online steganography tool—has an embedded message in it; have a look at whether you can spot any unusual patterns in the following image:

Most tools today can mask content within both complex and solid color images, to the point where, you as an end-user wouldn't even notice—as seen in the preceding example.

Continuing this scenario, a quick question you might need to answer right now is: does the file contain another file format within the file? Another element to consider is the scope of your question. Attempting to answer the aforementioned question would lead to a time-consuming deep dive into analyzing every file format used with a recursive parser—not something that would make sense to tackle right off the bat. A better option would be to scope the question to perhaps just analyze audio files or image files. Taking that thought process further, let's proceed by scoping the problem to a specific image type and payload type.

PNG image files with embedded executables

Let us dive into this more specific question: how can we detect Windows Executables within **Portable Network Graphics** (**PNG**) files? For those curious, the reasoning behind specifically choosing PNG files is that they are a very common lossless image format used in video games and the internet due to their great image quality-to-file size ratio. This level of usage creates an interface for attackers to get a PNG file on your machine, with you as the end user not thinking twice about it, versus a proprietary format or Windows **Executable** (**EXE**), which will likely cause alarm to the end user.

In the next section, we will break down the PNG file into the following steps:

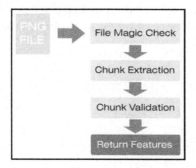

 To dive further into the PNG file format, the specification for PNG is available here: `http://libpng.org/pub/png/spec/1.2/PNG-Contents.html`

Creating a PNG parser

Let us now dive into taking apart the PNG file format into features in order to drive a potential model for detecting hidden payloads. A PNG file is structured with continuous chunks. Each chunk is composed of a header description field, followed by a payload of data. The chunks required for a PNG file include **IHDR, IDAT,** and **IEND**. The sections, as per the specification, must appear in that order. Each of these sections will be explained below.

The first element ahead of the chunks is to implement the check in order to make sure the file is actually a PNG image file. This check is generally called the **File Magic check**. The majority of files used throughout our digital world have a unique signature, making both the parsing and saving of these files easier.

 For those curious about other file format's signature, an extensive list can be found here: https://www.garykessler.net/library/file_sigs.html

PNG files specifically begin with the following bytes:

```
137, 80, 78, 71, 13, 10, 26, 10
```

By using these File Magic bytes, we can then utilize the SequenceEqual .NET method to compare the file data's first sequence of bytes, as shown in the following code:

```
using var ms = new MemoryStream(data);

byte[] fileMagic = new byte[FileMagicBytes.Length];

ms.Read(fileMagic, 0, fileMagic.Length);

if (!fileMagic.SequenceEqual(FileMagicBytes))
{
    return (string.Empty, false, null);
}
```

If the SequenceEqual method checks against the FileMagicBytes property and does not match, we return false. In this scenario, the file is not a PNG file, and therefore, we want to stop parsing the file any further.

From this point, we will now iterate over the chunks of the file. At any point, if the bytes aren't set properly, this should be noted, as Microsoft Paint or Adobe PhotoShop would save the file, as per the PNG file format's specification. A malicious generator, on the other hand, may bend the rules around adhering to the PNG file format's specification, as shown here:

```
while (ms.Position != data.Length)
{
    byte[] chunkInfo = new byte[ChunkInfoSize];

    ms.Read(chunkInfo, 0, chunkInfo.Length);

    var chunkSize = chunkInfo.ToInt32();

    byte[] chunkIdBytes = new byte[ChunkIdSize];

    ms.Read(chunkIdBytes, 0, ChunkIdSize);

    var chunkId = Encoding.UTF8.GetString(chunkIdBytes);

    byte[] chunk = new byte[chunkSize];

    ms.Read(chunk, 0, chunkSize);

    switch (chunkId)
    {
        case nameof(IHDR):
            var header = new IHDR(chunk);

            // Payload exceeds length
            if (data.Length <= (header.Width * header.Height *
                                MaxByteDepth) + ms.Position)
            {
                break;
            }

            return (FileType, false, new[] {"SUSPICIOUS: Payload is larger
                                than what the size should be" });
        case nameof(IDAT):
            // Build Embedded file from the chunks
            break;
        case nameof(IEND):
            // Note that the PNG had an end
            break;
    }
}
```

For each chunk, we read the `ChunkInfoSize` variable, which is defined as 4 bytes. This `ChunkInfoSize` array, once read, contains the size of the chunk to then read from. In addition to determining which chunk type we are to read, we also read the 4-byte chunk for the 4-character string (`IHDR`, `IDAT`, `IEND`).

Once we have the chunk size and the type, we then build out the class object representations of each. For the scope of this code example, we will just look at a snippet of the IHDR class, which contains the high-level image properties such as the dimensions, bit depth, and compression:

```
public class IHDR
{
    public Int32 Width;

    public Int32 Height;

    public byte BitDepth;

    public byte ColorType;

    public byte Compression;

    public byte FilterMethod;

    public byte Interlace;

    public IHDR(byte[] data)
    {
        Width = data.ToInt32();

        Height = data.ToInt32(4);
    }
}
```

We'll just pull the `Width` and `Height` properties, which are the first 8 bytes (4 bytes each). For this example, we also make use of an extension method to convert a byte array into an `Int32` array. IN most cases, BitConverter would be the ideal scenario, however, for this code example, I wanted to simplify the sequential accessing of data, such as the offset of 4 bytes when retrieving the previously mentioned `Height` property.

The previously mentioned IDAT chunks are the actual image data—and the potential chunk in which to contain the embedded payloads. The IEND, as the name implies, simply tells the PNG parser that the file is complete, that is, there is no payload in the IEND chunk.

Once the file has been parsed, we return the file type (**PNG**)—whether or not it is a validly structured PNG file—and we note anything that is suspicious, such as if the file size is considerably larger than it should be, given the width, height, and maximum bit depth (24). For each of these notes, they could be normalized, along with the valid/invalid flag in a production model. In addition, these could have a numeric representation with a simple enumeration.

> For those who are curious about the full application's source code, please refer to https://github.com/jcapellman/virus-tortoise, which utilizes many of the same principles that were shown in the *Creating the File Classification application* section of Chapter 9, *Using ML.NET with ASP.NET Core.*
>
> Taking this example a step further, to iterate through the IDAT chunks that contain the actual image data—and potential executable payloads—would complete the extractor in a production application.

Now that we have seen the required level of effort for building a production level of features, let us dive into building a production training dataset.

Obtaining training and testing datasets

Now that we have completed our discussion on feature engineering, the next step is to obtain a dataset. For some problems, this can be very difficult. For instance, when attempting to predict something that no one else has done, or that is in an emerging sector, having a training set to train on would be more difficult than say, finding malicious files for our previous example.

Another aspect to consider is diversity and how the data is broken out. For instance, consider how you would predict malicious Android applications based on behavioral analysis using the anomaly detection trainer that ML.NET provides. When thinking about building your dataset, most Android users, I would argue, do not have half of their apps as malicious. Therefore, an even malicious and benign (50/50) breakdown of training and test sets might be over-fitting on malicious applications. Figuring out and analyzing the actual representation of what your target users will encounter is critical, otherwise your model may either tend to a false positive or false negative, both of which your end users will not be happy with.

The last element to consider when training and testing datasets is how you are obtaining your datasets. Since your model is largely based on the training and test datasets, finding real datasets that represent your problem set is crucial. Using the previous steganography example, if you pulled random PNG files without validation, there is a possibility of training a model on bad data. A mitigation for this would be to check for hidden payloads within the IDAT chunks. Likewise, validation in the PNG example on the actual files is critical, as well. Training on JPG, BMP, or GIF files mixed in with your PNG files when you only run against PNG files in your production app could lead to false positives or negatives, as well. Because the binary structures of the other image formats differ from PNG, this non-representative data will skew the training set toward the unsupported formats.

 For those in the cyber-security field, VirusTotal (`https://www.virustotal.com`) and Reversing Labs (`https://www.reversinglabs.com`) offer extensive databases of files to download for a fee if local sources of data for various file types prove difficult to obtain.

Creating your model-building pipeline

Once your feature extractor has been created and your dataset obtained, the next element to establish is a model building pipeline. The definition of the model building pipeline can be shown better in the following diagram:

For each of the steps, we will discuss how they relate to the pipeline that you choose in the next section.

Discussing attributes to consider in a pipeline platform

There are quite a few pipeline tools that are available for deployment on-premises, both in the cloud and as **SaaS (Software as a Service)** services. We will review a few of the more commonly used platforms in the industry. However, the following points are a few elements to keep in mind, no matter which platform you choose:

- **Speed** is important for several reasons. While building your initial model, the time to iterate is very important, as you will more than likely be adjusting your training set and hyper-parameters in order to test various combinations. On the other end of the process, when you are in pre-production or production, the time to iterate with testers or customers (who are awaiting a new model in order to address issues or add features) is critical in most cases.

- **Repeatability** is also important to ensure that a perfect model can be rebuilt every time, given the same dataset, features, and hyper-parameters. Utilizing automation as much as possible is one method to avoid the human-error aspect of training models, while also helping the repeatability aspect. All of the platforms that will be reviewed in the next section promote defining a pipeline without any human input after launching a new training session.

- **Versioning and tracking of comparisons** are important in order to ensure that when changes are made, they can be compared. For example, whether it is hyper-parameters—such as the depth of your trees in a FastTree model—or additional samples that you add, keeping track of these changes as you iterate is critical. Hypothetically, if you made a documented change and your efficacy drops significantly, you could always go back and evaluate that one change. If you hadn't versioned or documented your individual changes for comparisons, this simple change could be very difficult to pinpoint the drop in efficacy. Another element of tracking is to track progress over a period of time, such as per quarter or per year. This level of tracking can help to paint a picture and can also help to drive the next steps or track trends in efficacy in order to obtain more samples or add additional features.

- Lastly, **quality assurance** is important for several reasons, and, in almost every case, critical to the success or failure of a project. Imagine a model being deployed straight to production without any extra checks being put in place by a dedicated quality assurance team performing manual and automated tests. Automated tests—as simple as a set of unit tests to ensure that samples test the same, or better, from model to model prior to release, and then to production—can be a good stop-gap solution instead of an entire automated suite of tests with specific ranges of efficacy to keep within.

All four of these elements should be considered when performing each step in the model building pipeline that was discussed in the previous section. The last step of delivery depends on the previous three elements being completed properly. The actual delivery is dependent on your application. For instance, if you're creating an ASP.NET application, such as the one that we created in Chapter 9, *Using ML.NET with ASP.NET Core*, adding the ML.NET model as part of your Jenkins pipeline—so that it automatically gets bundled with your deployment—would be a good approach.

Exploring machine learning platforms

The following are platforms I have either personally used, and/or had colleagues utilize in order to solve various problems. Each platform has its pros and cons, especially given the uniqueness of each problem that we are trying to solve.

Azure Machine Learning

Microsoft's Azure Cloud Platform provides a complete platform for Kubernetes, virtual machines, and databases, in addition to providing a machine learning platform. This platform provides direct connections to Azure SQL databases, Azure File Storage, and public URLs, to name just a few for training and test sets. A lightweight version that doesn't scale is provided inside of Visual Studio Community 2019 for free. The following screenshot shows the full-fledged UI:

In addition, non-.NET technologies, such as TensorFlow, PyTorch, and scikit-learn are fully supported. Tools such as the popular Jupyter Notebook and Azure Notebook are also fully supported.

Similar to Apache Airflow, reviewing run histories in order to compare versions is also easy to do in Azure Machine Learning.

All phases of the aforementioned model building pipeline are supported. Here are some of the pros and cons of Azure Machine Learning:

Pros:

- Extensive integrations into multiple data sources
- ML.NET natively supported
- Can scale up and down depending on your needs
- No infrastructure setup required

Cons:

- Can be expensive when training

Apache Airflow

Apache Airflow, an open source software, provides the ability to create pipelines of almost unlimited complexity. While not a natively supported framework, .NET Core applications—such as those that we have created throughout this book—can run, provided the .NET Core runtime is installed or simply compiled with the self-contained flags. While the learning curve is higher than Microsoft's Azure Machine Learning platform, being free in certain scenarios, especially when simply experimenting, might be more beneficial. The following screenshot shows the UI of Airflow:

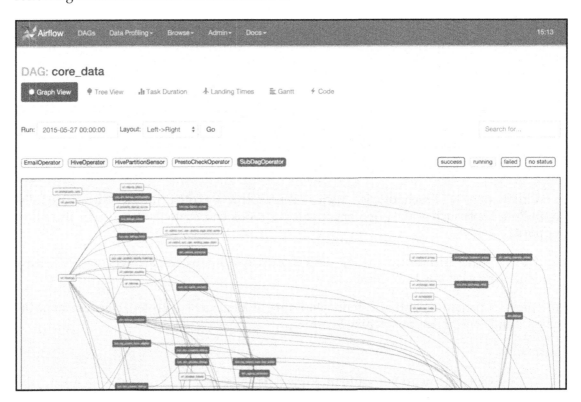

Much like Azure Machine Learning, the visualization of the pipelines does make the configuration of a particular pipeline easier than Apache Spark. However, much like Apache Spark, the setup and configuration (depending on your skill level) can be quite daunting, especially following the pip installation. An easier path to get up and running is by using a pre-built Docker container, such as Puckel's Docker container (`https://hub.docker.com/r/puckel/docker-airflow`).

Here are some of the pros and cons of Apache Airflow:

Pros:

- Free and open source
- Documentation and examples given the 4+ years
- Runs on Windows, Linux, and macOS

Cons:

- Complex to set up (especially with the official pip instructions)
- .NET is not natively supported

Apache Spark

Apache Spark, another open source tool, while generally used in big-data pipelines, can also be configured for feature extraction, training, and the production of models at scale. When memory and CPU constraints are hindering your ability to build models, for example, training with a massive dataset, I have personally seen Apache Spark scale to utilizing multiple 64C/128T AMD servers with over a terabyte of ram being maximized. I found this platform to be more difficult to set up than Apache Airflow or Azure's Machine Learning platform, however, once set up it can be quite powerful. The following screenshot shows the UI of Apache Spark:

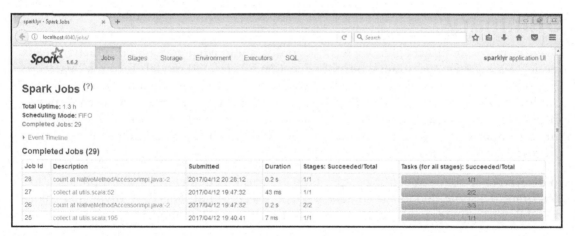

A great step by step install guide can be found on Microsoft's Apache Spark page (https://dotnet.microsoft.com/learn/data/spark-tutorial/intro) for both Windows and Linux. This guide does remove some of the unknowns, however, compared to Azure or Airflow it is still far from easy to get up and running. Here are some of the pros and cons of Apache Spark:

Pros:

- Free and open source
- .NET bindings from Microsoft
- Lots of documentation due to its long history (> 5 years old)
- Runs on Windows, macOS, and Linux

Cons:

- Can be difficult to configure and get up and running
- Sensitive to IT infrastructure changes

 Microsoft has written a .NET binding for Apache Spark and released it for free: https://dotnet.microsoft.com/apps/data/spark. These bindings are available for Windows, macOS, and Linux.

Summary

Over the course of this chapter, we have deep-dived into what goes into production-ready model training from the original purpose question to a trained model. Through this deep dive, we have examined the level of effort that is needed to create detailed features through production thought processes and feature engineering. We then reviewed the challenges, the ways to address the training, and how to test dataset questions. Lastly, we also dove into the importance of an actual model building pipeline, using an entirely automated process.

In the next chapter, we will utilize a pre-built TensorFlow model in a WPF application to determine if a submitted image contains certain objects or not. This deep dive will explore how ML.NET provides an easy-to-use interface for TensorFlow models.

Using TensorFlow with ML.NET

12

In this chapter, we will be using a pre-trained TensorFlow model, specifically the Inception model, and we'll integrate the model into a **Windows Presentation Foundation (WPF)** application. We will be taking the pre-trained model and applying transfer learning, by adding some pictures of food and bodies of water. After the transfer learning has been performed, we then allow the user to select their own images. By the end of the chapter, you should have a firm grasp of what it takes to integrate a TensorFlow model into your ML.NET application.

The following topics will be covered in this chapter:

- Breaking down Google's Inception model
- Creating the image classification desktop application
- Exploring additional production application enhancements

Breaking down Google's Inception model

Google's Inception model (`https://github.com/google/inception`) has been trained on millions of images to help with one of the growing questions in our society—what is in my image? The type of applications wanting to answer this question range from matching faces, automatically detecting weapons or unwanted objects, sports branding in game pictures (such as the brand of sneakers), and image archivers that provide users with the support they need to search without manual tags, to name just a few.

This type of question is typically answered with **object recognition**. An application of object recognition that you might already be familiar with is **optical character recognition (OCR)**. OCR is when an image of characters can be interpreted as text, such as what is found in Microsoft's OneNote Handwriting to Text feature, or in a toll booth that reads license plates. The particular application of object recognition that we will be looking into specifically is called **image classification**.

The Inception model helps with this problem by using deep learning to classify images. The model was trained in a supervised approach on millions of images, with the output being a neural network. The advantage of this approach is that the pre-built model can be enhanced with a smaller subset of images, which is what we will be doing in the next section of this chapter. This approach of adding additional data and labels is called **transfer learning**. This approach can also be helpful when creating customer-specific models.

Think of it like creating a branch from your master branch in GitHub; you might want to just add one class or modify one element without having to re-create the entire code base. In regards to models, take for instance, an image classifier for automobiles. Let us assume that you obtain millions of images covering US and foreign cars, trucks, vans, and more. A new customer comes to you requesting you to create a model to help monitor vehicles entering a government facility. The previous model should not be thrown away and won't need to be fully retrained, simply adding more commercial (or maybe military) vehicles with labels would be needed.

 For a larger and more in-depth deep dive into Google's image classification, a good resource is their developer documentation, which can be found from https://developers.google.com/machine-learning/practica/image-classification/.

Creating the WPF image classification application

As mentioned earlier, the application that we will be creating is an image classification application, specifically allowing the user to select an image and determine whether it is either food or water. This is achieved through the aforementioned and included, pre-trained TensorFlow Inception model. The first time that the application is run, the ML.NET version of the model is trained with the images and the tags.tsv file (to be reviewed in the next section).

As with previous chapters, the completed project code, sample dataset, and project files can be downloaded here: https://github.com/PacktPublishing/Hands-On-Machine-Learning-With-ML.NET/tree/master/chapter12.

Exploring the project architecture

In this chapter, we will dive into a WPF desktop application. As mentioned in the first section of this chapter, we will be using the WPF framework to create our application. You might be asking, why not a UWP application such as the browser application that we created in `Chapter 10`, *Using ML.NET with UWP*? The reasoning, at least at the time of writing, is that TensorFlow support, specifically for image classification, is not fully supported in a UWP application. Perhaps, in future versions of ML.NET, this will be added. For other non-image-based applications, you may be able to use TensorFlow in a UWP application.

Those who have done WPF development previously, and are looking closely, will notice that the project utilizes .NET Core 3.1. In .NET Core 3.0, Microsoft added support for WPF and WinForms, therefore, you are no longer tied to the Windows-only .NET Framework for GUI development. Instead, this support is added through the `Microsoft.WindowsDesktop.App.WPF` NuGet package.

For this example, we will be using the `Microsoft.ML` (1.3.1) NuGet package—in addition to several additional NuGet packages—to be able to utilize TensorFlow within our .NET application. These include the following:

- `Microsoft.ML.ImageAnalytics` (1.3.1)
- `Microsoft.ML.TensorFlow` (1.3.1)
- `SciSharp.TensorFlow.Redist` (1.14.0)

By the time you are reading this, there may very well be newer versions of the packages and they should work, however, the versions that were noted above are the ones that we are going to use in this deep dive, and what is available in the GitHub repository.

In the following screenshot, you will find the Visual Studio Solution Explorer view of the solution. Due to the TensorFlow support being much more particular about project types and CPU targets, we have gone back to a single project, as opposed to the three-project architecture that was used in the previous several chapters:

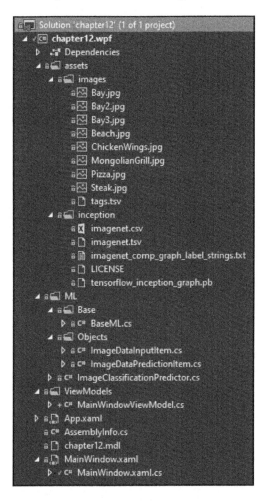

The tags.tsv file (found in the assets\images folder in the code repository) contains eight rows, which map the included images to the preclassification:

```
ChickenWings.jpg food
Steak.jpg food
Pizza.jpg food
MongolianGrill.jpg food
Bay.jpg water
```

```
Bay2.jpg water
Bay3.jpg water
Beach.jpg water
```

If you want to experiment with your own classification, delete the included images, copy your images, and update the `tags.tsv` file with the label. I should note, all of the images that are included were taken by me on various vacations to California—feel free to use them as you wish.

The files in the `assets/inception` folder contain all of the Google pre-trained files (and license file).

Diving into the WPF image classification application

As discussed in the opening section, our desktop application is a WPF application. For the scope of this example, as found in `Chapter 10`, *Using ML.NET with UWP*, we are using standard approaches for handling the application architecture by following the **Model-View-ViewModel (MVVM)** design pattern.

The files that we will be diving into in this section are as follows:

- `MainWindowViewModel`
- `MainWindow.xaml`
- `MainWindow.xaml.cs`
- `BaseML`
- `ImageDataInputItem`
- `ImageDataPredictionItem`
- `ImageClassificationPredictor`

The rest of the files inside the WPF project were untouched from the default Visual Studio .NET Core 3.1 WPF application template; for example, the `App.xaml` and `AssemblyInfo.cs` files.

The MainWindowViewModel class

The purpose of the `MainWindowViewModel` class is to contain our business logic and control the view, as shown here:

1. The first thing we do is instantiate our previously discussed `ImageClassificationPredictor` class, so that it can be used to run predictions:

```
private readonly ImageClassificationPredictor _prediction = new
ImageClassificationPredictor();
```

2. The next block of code handles the power of MVVM for the classification string, and also stores the selected image. For each of these properties, we call `OnPropertyChanged` upon a change in values, which triggers the binding of the View to refresh for any field that is bound to these properties:

```
private string _imageClassification;

public string ImageClassification
{
    get => _imageClassification;

    set
    {
        _imageClassification = value;
        OnPropertyChanged();
    }
}

private ImageSource _imageSource;

public ImageSource SelectedImageSource
{
    get => _imageSource;

    set
    {
        _imageSource = value;
        OnPropertyChanged();
    }
}
```

3. Next, we define the `Initialize` method, which calls the predictor's `Initialize` method. The method will return a tuple, which indicates whether the model can't be loaded or whether it is not found, along with the exception (if thrown):

```
public (bool Success, string Exception) Initialize() =>
_prediction.Initialize();
```

4. Then, we handle what happens when the user clicks the **Select Image** button. This method opens a dialog box prompting the user to select an image. If the user cancels the dialog, the method returns. Otherwise, we call the two helper methods to load the image into memory and classify the image:

```
public void SelectFile()
{
    var ofd = new OpenFileDialog
    {
        Filter = "Image Files(*.BMP;*.JPG;*.PNG)|*.BMP;*.JPG;*.PNG"
    };

    var result = ofd.ShowDialog();

    if (!result.HasValue || !result.Value)
    {
        return;
    }

    LoadImageBytes(ofd.FileName);

    Classify(ofd.FileName);
}
```

5. The `LoadImageBytes` method takes the filename and loads the image into our MVVM-based `ImageSource` property so, after selection, the image control is automatically updated to a view of the selected image:

```
private void LoadImageBytes(string fileName)
{
    var image = new BitmapImage();

    var imageData = File.ReadAllBytes(fileName);

    using (var mem = new MemoryStream(imageData))
    {
        mem.Position = 0;

        image.BeginInit();
```

```
            image.CreateOptions =
                    BitmapCreateOptions.PreservePixelFormat;
            image.CacheOption = BitmapCacheOption.OnLoad;
            image.UriSource = null;
            image.StreamSource = mem;
            image.EndInit();
        }

        image.Freeze();

        SelectedImageSource = image;
    }
```

6. And lastly, the `Classify` method takes the path and passes it into the `Predictor` class. Upon returning the prediction, the classification and confidence are built into our MVVM `ImageClassification` property, therefore, the UI is updated automatically:

```
public void Classify(string imagePath)
{
 var result = _prediction.Predict(imagePath);

 ImageClassification = $"Image ({imagePath}) is a picture of
 {result.PredictedLabelValue} with a confidence of
 {result.Score.Max().ToString("P2")}";
}
```

The last element of the `MainWindowViewModel` class is the same `OnPropertyChanged` method that we defined in Chapter 10, *Using ML.NET with UWP*, which allows the MVVM magic to happen. With our `ViewModel` class defined, let us move on to the `MainWindow` XAML file.

The MainWindow.xaml class

As discussed in the *Breaking down UWP architecture* section of Chapter 10, *Using ML.NET with UWP*, when describing the development, XAML markup is used to define your user interface. For the scope of this application, our UI is relatively simple: `Button`, `Image Control`, and `TextBlock`.

We will look at the code now:

1. The first thing that we define is our grid. In XAML, a grid is a container similar to a <div> in web development. We then define our rows. Similar to Bootstrap (but easier to understand in my opinion), is the pre-definition of the height of each row. Setting a row to `Auto` will auto-size the height to the content's height, while an asterisk translates to using all remaining height based on the main container's height:

```
<Grid.RowDefinitions>
    <RowDefinition Height="Auto" />
    <RowDefinition Height="*" />
    <RowDefinition Height="Auto" />
</Grid.RowDefinitions>
```

2. We first define our `Button` object, which will trigger the aforementioned `SelectFile` method in our `ViewModel` class:

```
<Button Grid.Row="0" Margin="0,10,0,0" Width="200" Height="35"
Content="Select Image File" HorizontalAlignment="Center"
Click="btnSelectFile_Click" />
```

3. We then define our `Image` control, which is bound to our previously reviewed `SelectedImageSource` property that is found in our `ViewModel` class:

```
<Image Grid.Row="1" Margin="10,10,10,10" Source="{Binding
SelectedImageSource}" />
```

4. We then add the `TextBlock` control that will display our classification:

```
<TextBlock Grid.Row="2" Text="{Binding ImageClassification,
Mode=OneWay}" TextWrapping="Wrap" Foreground="White"
Margin="10,10,10,10" HorizontalAlignment="Center" FontSize="16" />
```

With the XAML aspect of our View defined, let us now dive into the code behind of the `MainWindow` class.

The MainWindow.xaml.cs file

The `MainWindow.xaml.cs` file contains the code behind the XAML view, which is discussed here:

1. The first thing that we define is a wrapper property around the `DataContext` property, which is built into the base `Window` class:

```
private MainWindowViewModel ViewModel => (MainWindowViewModel)
DataContext;
```

2. Next, we define the constructor for `MainWindow`, in order to initialize the `DataContext` property to our `MainWindowViewModel` object. If the initialization fails, we do not want the application to continue. In addition, we need to let the user know why it failed, using a `MessageBox` object:

```
public MainWindow()
{
    InitializeComponent();

    DataContext = new MainWindowViewModel();

    var (success, exception) = ViewModel.Initialize();

    if (success)
    {
        return;
    }

    MessageBox.Show($"Failed to initialize model - {exception}");

    Application.Current.Shutdown();
}
```

3. Lastly, we call the ViewModel's `SelectFile` method to handle the image selection and classification:

```
private void btnSelectFile_Click(object sender, RoutedEventArgs e)
=> ViewModel.SelectFile();
```

With the code behind of the `MainWindow` class behind us, that concludes the WPF component. Let us now focus on the machine learning part of the example.

The BaseML class

The BaseML class, as used in most of the previous examples, exposes a base class for our ML.NET classes. In the case of this example, we actually streamlined the class due to the nature of using a pre-trained model. The class now simply initializes the MLContext property:

```
public class BaseML
{
    protected MLContext MlContext;

    public BaseML()
    {
        MlContext = new MLContext(2020);
    }
}
```

With the streamlined BaseML class reviewed, let us dive into the ImageDataInputItem class.

The ImageDataInputItem class

The ImageDataInputItem class contains our class to pass into the model; the essential property is the ImagePath property:

```
public class ImageDataInputItem
{
    [LoadColumn(0)]
    public string ImagePath;

    [LoadColumn(1)]
    public string Label;
}
```

While smaller than most of our input classes, the Inception model only requires the two properties. Now, let us dive into the output class that is called ImageDataPredictionItem.

The ImageDataPredictionItem class

The `ImageDataPredictionItem` class contains the prediction response, including the confidence of the predicted value string (to contain `Water` or `Food` in the case of the included images):

```
public class ImageDataPredictionItem : ImageDataInputItem
{
    public float[] Score;

    public string PredictedLabelValue;
}
```

Much like the input class, the output class has only two properties, similar to previous examples. With the input and output classes behind us, let us dive into the `ImageClassificationPredictor` class, which uses these classes for transfer learning and predictions.

The ImageClassificationPredictor class

The `ImageClassificationPredictor` class contains all of the code that is needed to load and predict against the Inception TensorFlow model:

1. First, we need to define several helper variables to access the images and `.tsv` files:

```
// Training Variables
private static readonly string _assetsPath =
    Path.Combine(Environment.CurrentDirectory, "assets");
private static readonly string _imagesFolder =
    Path.Combine(_assetsPath, "images");
private readonly string _trainTagsTsv =
    Path.Combine(_imagesFolder, "tags.tsv");
private readonly string _inceptionTensorFlowModel =
    Path.Combine(_assetsPath, "inception",
                 "tensorflow_inception_graph.pb");

private const string TF_SOFTMAX = "softmax2_pre_activation";
private const string INPUT = "input";

private static readonly string ML_NET_MODEL =
    Path.Combine(Environment.CurrentDirectory, "chapter12.mdl");
```

2. Next, we define the settings that the pre-trained Inception model needs:

```
private struct InceptionSettings
{
    public const int ImageHeight = 224;
    public const int ImageWidth = 224;
    public const float Mean = 117;
    public const float Scale = 1;
    public const bool ChannelsLast = true;
}
```

3. Next, we create our `Predict` method and overload that simply takes the image file path. Like in previous examples, we create `PredictionEngine` with a call to our `MLContext` object, passing in our input class (`ImageDataInputItem`) and our output class (`ImageDataPredictionItem`), and then calling the `Predict` method to get our model prediction:

```
public ImageDataPredictionItem Predict(string filePath) =>
    Predict(new ImageDataInputItem
        {
            ImagePath = filePath
        }
    );

public ImageDataPredictionItem Predict(ImageDataInputItem image)
{
    var predictor = MlContext.Model.CreatePredictionEngine
        <ImageDataInputItem, ImageDataPredictionItem>(_model);

    return predictor.Predict(image);
}
```

4. Finally, we initialize and extend our pre-trained model with our own samples:

```
public (bool Success, string Exception) Initialize()
{
    try
    {
        if (File.Exists(ML_NET_MODEL))
        {
            _model = MlContext.Model.Load(ML_NET_MODEL,
                            out DataViewSchema modelSchema);

            return (true, string.Empty);
        }

        ...
```

```
    }
    catch (Exception ex)
    {
        return (false, ex.ToString());
    }
}
```

For the full code, please refer to the following GitHub repository link: `https://github.com/PacktPublishing/Hands-On-Machine-Learning-With-ML.NET/blob/master/chapter12/chapter12.wpf/ML/ImageClassificationPredictor.cs`. With the `Initialize` method completed, that concludes the code deep dive. Let us now run the application!

Running the image classification application

Since we are using a pre-trained model, we can just run the application from Visual Studio. Upon running the application, you will be presented with a mostly empty window:

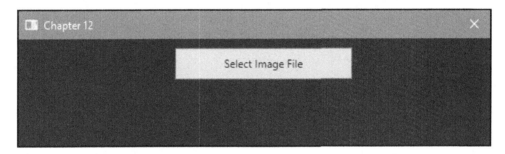

Clicking on the **Select Image File** button and then selecting an image file will trigger the model to run. In my case, I selected a picture from a recent vacation to Germany, which came back with a 98.84% confidence score:

Feel free to try various files on your machine to see the confidence score and classification—if you start noticing issues, add more samples to the images folder and `tags.tsv` file, as noted in the earlier section. Be sure to delete the `chapter12.mdl` file prior to making these changes.

Additional ideas for improvements

Now that we have completed our deep dive, there are a couple of additional elements that could possibly further enhance the application. A few ideas are discussed here.

Self-training based on the end user's input

One of the advantages, as noted in the opening section of this chapter, is the ability to utilize transfer learning in dynamic applications. Unlike previous example applications that have been reviewed in this book, this application could actually allow the end user to select a series (or folder) of images, and with a few code changes, build the new `.tsv` file and train a new model. For a web application or commercial product, this would provide a high value and would also reduce the burden on you to, for instance, obtain images of every type—a daunting, and more than likely futile, goal.

Logging

As mentioned in the *Logging* section of `Chapter 10`, *Using ML.NET with UWP*, having a desktop application has its pros and cons. The biggest con necessitating the need for logging is that your desktop application could be installed on any number of configurations of Windows 7 to Windows 10, with an almost unlimited number of permutations. As mentioned previously, logging by utilizing NLog (`https://nlog-project.org/`) or a similar open source project is highly recommended, coupled with a remote logging solution such as Loggly, so that you can get error data from your user's machines. Given the GDPR and recent CCPA, we need to ensure that the data that is leaving the end user's machines is conveyed and that these logs do not include personal data (or actual images uploaded to a remote server via the logging mechanism).

Utilizing a database

Similar to the performance optimization suggestion in `Chapter 10`, *Using ML.NET with UWP*, if a user selects the same image more than once, especially if this application was being used in a kiosk or converted to a web application, the performance advantages of storing the classification could be fairly significant. A quick and easy method for achieving this could be to perform a SHA256 of the image, and check that hash against a database. Depending on the number of users and if they are going to be concurrent, I would suggest one of two options:

- If the users are going one at a time and the application is going to remain a WPF application, using the previously mentioned lightweight database—LiteDB (`http://www.litedb.org/`)—would be recommended.
- If you are launching a large web application using a production, then MongoDB or a horizontally scalable database, such as Microsoft's CosmosDB would be recommended in order to ensure that the database lookups wouldn't be slower than simply re-performing the model prediction.

Summary

Over the course of this chapter, we have deep-dived into what goes into creating a WPF application using a pre-trained TensorFlow model. We also reviewed and looked closely into Google's image classification Inception model. In addition, we learned how to take that model and integrate it in order to perform image classification on user-selected images. Lastly, we also discussed some ways to further enhance the example application.

In the next and last chapter, we will focus on using a pre-trained ONNX model in a WPF application for object detection.

Using ONNX with ML.NET

13

Now that we have completed our deep dive into using TensorFlow with a **Windows Presentation Foundation (WPF)** application and ML.NET, it is now time to dive into using **Open Neural Network eXchange (ONNX)** with ML.NET. Specifically, in this final chapter, we will review what ONNX is, in addition to creating a new example application with a pre-trained ONNX model called **YOLO**. This application will build on the previous chapter and show the bounding boxes of the objects that the model detects. In addition, we will close out the chapter with suggestions on improving the example, for it to either become a production-grade application or be integrated into a production application.

In this chapter, we will cover the following topics:

- Breaking down ONNX and YOLO
- Creating the ONNX object detection application
- Exploring additional production application enhancements

Breaking down ONNX and YOLO

As mentioned in Chapter 1, *Getting Started with Machine Learning and ML.NET*, the ONNX standard is widely regarded within the industry as a truly universal format across machine learning frameworks. In the next two sections, we will review what ONNX provides, in addition to the YOLO model that will drive our example in this chapter.

Introducing ONNX

ONNX was created as a way for a less locked-down and free-flowing process when working with either pre-trained models or training models across frameworks. By providing an open format for frameworks to export to, ONNX allows interoperability, and thereby promotes experimentation that would have otherwise been prohibitive due to the nature of proprietary formats being used in almost every framework.

Currently, supported frameworks include TensorFlow, XGBoost, and PyTorch—in addition to ML.NET, of course.

If you want to deep dive into ONNX further, please check out their website: `https://onnx.ai/index.html`.

The YOLO ONNX model

Building on the work that was performed in `Chapter 12`, *TensorFlow with ML.NET*, in which we used the pre-trained Inception model, in this chapter, we are going to use the pre-trained YOLO model. This model provides very fast and accurate object detection, meaning it can find multiple objects within an image with a certain level of confidence. This differs from the last chapter's model that provided a pure image classification, such as water or food.

To help visualize the difference between the two models, take the previous chapter's TensorFlow model that classified water, and compare that to this chapter's object detection of a car, as illustrated in the following screenshot:

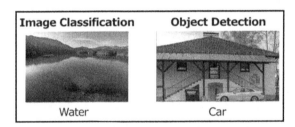

Object detection within images (and video) has been increasing in demand due to the significantly increased amount of images on the internet and the need for security. Imagine a crowded environment such as a football stadium, in particular by the front gates. Security guards patrol and monitor this area; however, like you, they are only human and can only glance at so many people with a certain level of accuracy. Applying object detection with machine learning in real time to pick up on weapons or large bags could then be used to alert the security guards to go after a suspect.

The YOLO model itself comes in two main forms—a tiny and a full model. For the scope of this example, we will be using the smaller of the models (~60 MB) that can classify 20 objects found within an image. The tiny model is comprised of nine convolutional layers and six max-pooling layers. The full model can classify thousands of objects and, given the proper hardware (namely, **graphics processing units (GPUs)**), can run faster than real-time.

The following diagram depicts how the YOLO model works (and neural networks, to a degree):

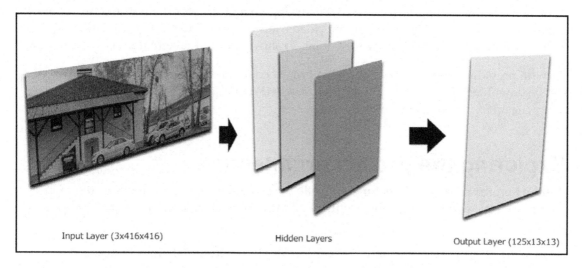

Input Layer (3x416x416)   Hidden Layers   Output Layer (125x13x13)

Effectively, the image (or images) is converted to 3 x 416 x 416 images. The 3 component represents the **Red-Green-Blue (RGB)** values. Consider the darkest layer as the red one, and the green layer as the lightest. The 416 values represent the width and height of the resized image. This input layer is then inputted into the hidden layers of the model. For the Tiny YOLO v2 model that we are using in this chapter, there are a total of 15 layers before outputting the layer.

To deep dive further into the YOLO model, please read this paper:
`https://arxiv.org/pdf/1612.08242.pdf`.

Creating the ONNX object detection application

As mentioned earlier, the application we will be creating is an object detection application using a pre-trained ONNX model. Using the application we developed in Chapter 12, *Using TensorFlow with ML.NET* as a starting point, we will add in support for bounding boxes overlaid on top of the image when the model categorizes objects of which it is aware. The usefulness of this to the general public is in the various applications image object detection provides. Imagine that you are working on a project for the police or intelligence community, where they have images or videos and want to detect weapons. Utilizing the YOLO model with ML.NET, as we are going to show, would make that process very easy.

As with previous chapters, the completed project code, pre-trained model, and project files can be downloaded here: https://github.com/PacktPublishing/Hands-On-Machine-Learning-With-ML.NET/tree/master/chapter13.

Exploring the project architecture

Building on the project architecture and code we created in previous chapters, the architecture we will be reviewing is enhanced to be more structured and usable by an end user.

As in some of the previous chapters, the following two additional NuGet packages are required if you want to utilize an ONNX model and perform object detection:

- Microsoft.ML.ImageAnalytics
- Microsoft.ML.OnnxTransformer

These NuGet packages are already referenced in the included sample code. Version 1.3.1 of these packages is used in both the included example on GitHub and throughout this chapter's deep dive.

In the following screenshot, you will find the Visual Studio Solution Explorer view of the project. There are several new additions to the solution, to facilitate the production use case we are targeting. We will review in detail each of the new files in the following solution screenshot later on in this chapter:

Due to a current ML.NET limitation as of this writing, ONNX support is only provided for scoring using a pre-existing model. The pre-trained model included in this example can be found in the `assets/model` folder.

Diving into the code

For this application, as noted in the previous section, we are building on top of the work completed in `Chapter 12`, *Using TensorFlow with ML.NET*. While the **user interface** (**UI**) has not changed much, the underlying code to run an ONNX model has. For each file changed—as in previous chapters—we will review the changes made and the reasoning behind the changes.

Classes that were changed or added are as follows:

- `DimensionsBase`
- `BoundingBoxDimensions`
- `YoloBoundingBox`
- `MainWindow.xaml`
- `ImageClassificationPredictor`
- `MainWindowViewModel`

There is one additional file, with the `YoloOutputParser` class contained within. This class is derived from the **Massachusetts Institute of Technology (MIT)** licensed interface for the `TinyYOLO` ONNX model. Due to the length of this class, we will not review it; however, the code does read easily, and if you wish to step through a prediction, the flow will be easy to follow.

The DimensionsBase class

The `DimensionsBase` class contains the coordinates along with the `Height` and `Width` properties, as illustrated in the following code block:

```
public class DimensionsBase
{
    public float X { get; set; }

    public float Y { get; set; }
    public float Height { get; set; }
    public float Width { get; set; }
}
```

This base class is used by both the `YoloOutputParser` and `BoundingBoxDimensions` classes to reduce code duplication.

The YoloBoundingBox class

The `YoloBoundingBox` class provides the container class for what is used to populate our bounding boxes when generating them for the overlay, as illustrated in the following code block:

```
public class YoloBoundingBox
{
    public BoundingBoxDimensions Dimensions { get; set; }
```

```
    public string Label { get; set; }

    public float Confidence { get; set; }

    public RectangleF Rect => new RectangleF(Dimensions.X, Dimensions.Y,
                                    Dimensions.Width, Dimensions.Height);

    public Color BoxColor { get; set; }
}
```

In addition, also defined in this same class file is our BoundingBoxDimensions class, as shown in the following code block:

```
public class BoundingBoxDimensions : DimensionsBase { }
```

Again, this inheritance is used to reduce code duplication.

The MainWindow.xaml file

The **Extensible Application Markup Language (XAML)** view of our application has been simplified to just the button and the image controls, as illustrated in the following code block:

```
<Grid>
    <Grid.RowDefinitions>
        <RowDefinition Height="Auto" />
        <RowDefinition Height="*" />
    </Grid.RowDefinitions>

    <Button Grid.Row="0" Margin="0,10,0,0" Width="200" Height="35"
     Content="Select Image File" HorizontalAlignment="Center"
     Click="btnSelectFile_Click" />

    <Image Grid.Row="1" Margin="10,10,10,10"
     Source="{Binding SelectedImageSource}" />
</Grid>
```

In addition, due to the nature of the bounding boxes and images you may select, the window has defaulted to Maximized, as can be seen in the following code block:

```
<Window x:Class="chapter13.wpf.MainWindow"
        xmlns="http://schemas.microsoft.com/winfx/2006/xaml/presentation"
        xmlns:x="http://schemas.microsoft.com/winfx/2006/xaml"
        xmlns:d="http://schemas.microsoft.com/expression/blend/2008"
        xmlns:mc=
            "http://schemas.openxmlformats.org/markup-compatibility/2006"
```

```
xmlns:local="clr-namespace:chapter13.wpf"
mc:Ignorable="d"
ResizeMode="NoResize"
WindowStyle="SingleBorderWindow"
WindowState="Maximized"
WindowStartupLocation="CenterScreen"
Background="#1e1e1e"
Title="Chapter 13" Height="450" Width="800">
```

With the XAML changes behind us, let us now dive into the revised
`ImageClassificationPredictor` class.

The ImageClassificationPredictor class

The `ImageClassificationPredictor` class, much like that of `Chapter 12`, *Using
TensorFlow with ML.NET*, contains the methods to run our image prediction. In this chapter,
we will need to make several additional class objects to support the running of an ONNX
model, as follows:

1. First, we define the `ImageNetSettings` struct that defines the height and width
   of our network. The YOLO model requires the use of 416 pixels by 416 pixels, as
   illustrated in the following code block:

   ```
   public struct ImageNetSettings
   {
       public const int imageHeight = 416;
       public const int imageWidth = 416;
   }
   ```

2. Next, we define the `TinyYoloModelSettings` struct to be used with the ONNX
   model, as follows:

   ```
   public struct TinyYoloModelSettings
   {
       public const string ModelInput = "image";

       public const string ModelOutput = "grid";
   }
   ```

3. Unlike the previous chapter, where the TensorFlow model was imported and then exported as an ML.NET model on the first run, ONNX, as of this writing, does not support that path. So, we must load the ONNX model in the `Initialize` method every time, as illustrated in the following code block:

```
public (bool Success, string Exception) Initialize()
{
    try
    {
        if (File.Exists(ML_NET_MODEL))
        {
            var data = MlContext.Data.LoadFromEnumerable(
                                new List<ImageDataInputItem>());

            var pipeline = MlContext.Transforms.LoadImages(
                outputColumnName: "image", imageFolder: "",
                inputColumnName: nameof(
                    ImageDataInputItem.ImagePath))
                .Append(MlContext.Transforms.ResizeImages(
                    outputColumnName: "image",
                    imageWidth: ImageNetSettings.imageWidth,
                    imageHeight: ImageNetSettings.imageHeight,
                    inputColumnName: "image"))
                .Append(MlContext.Transforms.ExtractPixels(
                    outputColumnName: "image"))
                .Append(MlContext.Transforms.ApplyOnnxModel(
                    modelFile: ML_NET_MODEL,
                    outputColumnNames: new[] {
                            TinyYoloModelSettings.ModelOutput},
                    inputColumnNames: new[] {
                            TinyYoloModelSettings.ModelInput}));

            _model = pipeline.Fit(data);

            return (true, string.Empty);
        }

        return (false, string.Empty);
    }
    catch (Exception ex)
    {
        return (false, ex.ToString());
    }
}
```

4. Next, we modify the `Predict` method extensively to support the `YoloParser` call, calling the `DrawBoundingBox` method to overlay the bounding boxes, and then returning the bytes of the updated image, as follows:

```
public byte[] Predict(string fileName)
{
    var imageDataView = MlContext.Data.LoadFromEnumerable(
        new List<ImageDataInputItem>{new ImageDataInputItem{
            ImagePath = fileName}});

    var scoredData = _model.Transform(imageDataView);

    var probabilities = scoredData.GetColumn<float[]>(
        TinyYoloModelSettings.ModelOutput);

    var parser = new YoloOutputParser();

    var boundingBoxes =
        probabilities
            .Select(probability =>
                parser.ParseOutputs(probability))
            .Select(boxes =>
                parser.FilterBoundingBoxes(boxes, 5, .5F));

    return DrawBoundingBox(fileName,
        boundingBoxes.FirstOrDefault());
}
```

For brevity, the `DrawBoundingBox` method is not shown here. At a high level, the original image is loaded into memory, and the model's bounding boxes are then drawn on top of the image, along with the label and confidence. This updated image is then converted to a byte array and returned.

The MainWindowViewModel class

Inside the `MainWindowViewModel` class, there are a couple of changes to be made due to the nature of the example. We look at them here:

1. First, the `LoadImageBytes` method now simply takes the parsed image bytes and converts them to an `Image` object, like this:

```
private void LoadImageBytes(byte[] parsedImageBytes)
{
    var image = new BitmapImage();
```

```
using (var mem = new MemoryStream(parsedImageBytes))
{
    mem.Position = 0;

    image.BeginInit();
    image.CreateOptions =
        BitmapCreateOptions.PreservePixelFormat;
    image.CacheOption = BitmapCacheOption.OnLoad;
    image.UriSource = null;
    image.StreamSource = mem;
    image.EndInit();
}

image.Freeze();

SelectedImageSource = image;
}
```

2. Lastly, we modify the `Classify` method to call the `LoadImageBytes` method upon successfully running the model, as follows:

```
public void Classify(string imagePath)
{
    var result = _prediction.Predict(imagePath);

    LoadImageBytes(result);
}
```

With the changes in place for the `Classify` method, that concludes the code changes required for this chapter's example. Now, let us run the application!

Running the application

To run the application, the process is identical to the sample application in `Chapter 12,` *Using TensorFlow with ML.NET*. To run the application from within Visual Studio, simply click the *play* icon found in the toolbar, as illustrated in the following screenshot:

After launching the application, just as in Chapter 12, *Using TensorFlow with ML.NET*, select an image file, and the model will run. For example, I selected an image I took on a vacation to Germany (note the car's bounding boxes), shown in the following screenshot:

Feel free to try selecting images you have on your hard drive to see the confidence level of the detection and how well the bounding boxes are formed around the objects.

Exploring additional production application enhancements

Now that we have completed our deep dive, there are a couple of additional elements to further enhance the application. A few ideas are discussed in the upcoming sections.

Logging

As noted previously, the importance of logging cannot be stressed enough within desktop applications. Logging utilizing NLog (`https://nlog-project.org/`) or a similar open-source project is highly recommended as your application complexity increases. This will allow you to log to a file, console, or third-party logging solution such as Loggly, at varying levels. For instance, if you deploy this application to a customer, breaking down the error level to at least Debug, Warning, and Error will be helpful when debugging issues remotely.

Image scaling

As you might have noticed, with images that are quite large (those exceeding your screen resolution), the text labeling of the bounding boxes and resizing within the image preview is not as easy to read as for, say, a 640 x 480 image. One area of improvement here would be to provide hover-over capabilities, resizing the image to the dimensions of the window or increasing the font size dynamically.

Utilizing the full YOLO model

In addition, another area of improvement for this sample would be to use the full YOLO model within an application. As previously noted with the Tiny YOLO model used within the example application, only 20 labels are provided. In a production application or one in which you wish to build on, using the larger, more complex model would be a good choice.

 You can download the full YOLO model here: `https://github.com/onnx/models/tree/master/vision/object_detection_segmentation/yolov3`.

Summary

Over the course of this chapter, we have deep dived into what goes into the ONNX format and what it offers to the community. In addition, we also created a brand new detection engine using the pre-trained Tiny YOLO model in ML.NET.

And with that, this concludes your deep dive into ML.NET. Between the first page of this book and this one, you have hopefully grown to understand the power that ML.NET offers in a very straightforward feature-rich abstraction. With ML.NET constantly evolving (much like .NET), there will be no doubt about the evolution of ML.NET's feature sets and deployment targets, ranging from embedded **Internet of Things** (**IoT**) devices to mobile devices. I hope this book was beneficial for your deep dive into ML.NET and machine learning. In addition, I hope that as you approach problems in the future, you will first think about whether the problem would benefit from utilizing ML.NET to solve the problem more efficiently and, potentially, better overall. Given the world's data continually growing at exponential rates, the necessity for using non-brute-force/traditional approaches will only continue to grow, therefore the skills garnered from this book should help you for years to come.

Other Books You May Enjoy

If you enjoyed this book, you may be interested in these other books by Packt:

C# Machine Learning Projects
Yoon Hyup Hwang

ISBN: 978-1-78899-640-2

- Set up the C# environment for machine learning with required packages
- Build classification models for spam email filtering
- Get to grips with feature engineering using NLP techniques for Twitter sentiment analysis
- Forecast foreign exchange rates using continuous and time-series data
- Make a recommendation model for music genre recommendation
- Familiarize yourself with munging image data and Neural Network models for handwritten-digit recognition
- Use Principal Component Analysis (PCA) for cyber attack detection
- One-Class Support Vector Machine for credit card fraud detection

Hands-On Machine Learning with C#
Matt R. Cole

ISBN: 978-1-78899-494-1

- Learn to parameterize a probabilistic problem
- Use Naive Bayes to visually plot and analyze data
- Plot a text-based representation of a decision tree using nuML
- Use the Accord.NET machine learning framework for associative rule-based learning
- Develop machine learning algorithms utilizing fuzzy logic
- Explore support vector machines for image recognition
- Understand dynamic time warping for sequence recognition

Leave a review - let other readers know what you think

Please share your thoughts on this book with others by leaving a review on the site that you bought it from. If you purchased the book from Amazon, please leave us an honest review on this book's Amazon page. This is vital so that other potential readers can see and use your unbiased opinion to make purchasing decisions, we can understand what our customers think about our products, and our authors can see your feedback on the title that they have worked with Packt to create. It will only take a few minutes of your time, but is valuable to other potential customers, our authors, and Packt. Thank you!

Index

Made in the USA
Monee, IL
19 November 2020